# HIDDEN In Plain Sight

The Parable of the
Moorish Sardine

by
Cush Dey

©2023
Califa Media Publishing

# Hidden in Plain Sight
## The Parable of the Moorish Sardine

© 2023
Califa Media Publishing
Lafayette, Indiana

by
Bro. Cush Dey

ISBN-13: 978-1-952828-89-8

All Rights Reserved. Without Prejudice. No Part Of This Book May Be Reproduced Or Transmitted In Any Form By Any Means, Electronic, Photocopying, Mechanical, Recording, Information Storage Or Retrieval System Unless For The Liberation Of Minds And Gaining Knowledge Of Self.

**COPYRIGHT DISCLAIMER**: *Under Sec.107 OF THE COPYRIGHT ACT OF 1976, allowance is made for "fair use" for purposes such as criticism, comment, news reporting, teaching, scholarship, and research. Fair use is permitted by copyright statute that might otherwise be infringing. Non-profit, educational, or personal use tips the balance in favor of fair use.*

Califa Media™
A Moorish Guide Publishing Company
califamedia.com
All Rights, Remedies & Liberties Reserved

Cover Design by Sis. T. Najee-Ullah El
Califa Media Publishing

# Table of Contents

**Editor's Note**
How to use this text................................................. i

**Moorish American Prayer** ........................................... ii

**Chapter One**
Moorish History IS History ................................... 1

**Chapter 2**
Man Know Thyself.............................................. 13

**Chapter 3**
AbraKaDaBra ...................................................... 29

**Chapter 4**
The Dangers of Color ......................................... 47

**Chapter 5**
What is Belief?.................................................... 69

**Chapter 6**
U.S CORPORATION ............................................. 81

**Chapter 7**
What Does Conversion Mean in Law?............. 101

**Other Titles from
Califa Media Publishing**........................................... 113

# Notes

# Editor's Note

## How to use this text

So that you may make most effective use to the instructions contained in this text, I encourage the reader to have close at hand the following:

- A good standard dictionary of the English language, preferably one printed before 1965. This dictionary is suggested as many definitions—especially those pertaining to our people—were altered after the Civil Rights Movement in the United States. An example would be comparing the definitions of "American" in a pre-1965 dictionary versus one printed more recently. Please note, there is no glossary contained in this guide to encourage use of the dictionary. Man—nor woman— knows not by being told.

- A Holy Quran of Mecca. The Prophet Noble Drew Ali did not release the Holy Koran of the Moorish Science Temple of America Circle Seven until between 1926 and 1928. The Moorish Holy Temple of Science, predecessor of the Moorish Science Temple of America, was founded in 1913 (Key 9). One must therefore ask themselves, what was the Prophet teaching from prior to the release of the Circle 7? The use of the Holy Quran of Mecca is further validated by its reference on our M.S.T. of A. Nationality Card: "I do hereby declare that you are a Moslem under the divine Laws of the Holy Koran of Mecca..."

- Holy Koran of the Moorish Science Temple of America Circle Seven.

- A bible of your choice.

As you read this text you will notice spaces along the outter edges of the pages. These are reserved for any notes you may wish to make. Scholarly works encourage the student to make notes next to the item being noted for quick future reference.

> Willing you much success in your endeavor to improve yourself, and thereby, our Nation.

Peace & Love

Sis. Tauheedah S. Najee-Ullah El
**Managing Editor**
**Califa Media Publishing**

# Moorish American Prayer

·····
## Allah

Father of the Universe, the Father
of Love, Truth, Peace, Freedom and Justice. ALLAH
is my Protection, my Guide and my Salvation By Night
and by Day, through Her Holy Prophet Noble Drew Ali.

·····
AMEN

# Chapter One

## Moorish History IS History

Sometimes the best place to hide something is right in front of our faces.

Questions to consider...

1. What is the first thing you think of when you hear about Moors?
2. What is a Moor/ Moorish American?
3. If nationality isn't important, why does everyone around the world except so called black, people of color, African Americans, Indians, Hebrews etc, claim one?
4. What has been the treatment of anyone claiming to be colorable misnomers?
5. Why has this Moorish history been hidden from humanity specifically in North, Central, South America and the adjoining islands?
6. Who are the Moors?
7. How significant is the Moorish contribution to civilization?
8. What does denationalization mean?
9. Who made you?
10. What have all the so-called black organizations done for so-called black people?

The purpose of this book is to present concrete evidence and irrefutable proof that Moorish History is in fact WORLD HISTORY.

## Let's Begin

*The Moors were enslaved by reducing their mentality to that of negros, blacks, and colored people. As a man thinketh so is he. Moors, you sleep too much. Wake up and see the seven bridges crossing the sky. Can you see you are a people?* -Noble Drew Ali

*Dogs and slaves were named by their master and only free man named themselves.* ~ Dr. John Henrik Clarke

*Elijah Muhammad spoke of on two men who were the forerunners to him: Noble Drew Ali was number one, and Marcus Garvey was number two.* ~ Minister Louis Farrakhan

*"The possession of knowledge, unless accompanied by a manifestation and expression in action, is like the hoarding of precious metals — a vain and a foolish thing knowledge, like wealth, is intended for use. The law of use is universal, and he who violates it suffers by reason of his conflict with natural forces."* ~The Kybalion

Due to deliberate indoctrination by the school systems, from grammar school to middle school, high school, and even in so-called "higher learning" institutions, there have been and continue to be silent weapons for quiet wars in full operation nationwide since 1913. This has resulted in widespread confusion, which in turn has led to feelings of anger, hatred, envy, mistreatment, and abuse, practiced and experienced generation after generation. This phenomenon can be identified as the deliberate reduction of knowledge and critical thinking abilities in humanity, particularly affecting the aboriginal and indigenous people of the land, namely the Moors.

To transform the conditions of civilization, individuals must reconnect with the mindset of their ancient foremothers and forefathers. This entails questioning everything they've been taught throughout their lives, and reexamining subjects like law, etymology, language, history, architecture, music, geometry, and astrology, just to name a few.

## Law

Law is a rule, an order, a pattern, a plan, or a system to which a phenomenon or action coexists or follows each other, in a phrase "cause and effect". Law relates in the science of observation to principles deduced from specific and particular facts, these facts being mathematical or scientific. Conclusions, cause and effect, etc., are put into words or statements that express those acquired facts, effects, or potentials for occurrences, if and when certain conditions are present.

The laws of the English language were purposefully ommitted by the school systems to instill confusion from early as kindergarten.

## Let's take a look at the 8 parts of speech:

Etymon, derived from the Latin word for "origin of a word," and the Greek word "etymon," which means the "literal meaning of a word" according to its origin. Have you ever heard the expression "getting to the root of the problem?" That would be the equivalent of etymon and etymology. This concept MUST be understood for effective change to occur.

### Parts of Speech chart with Examples

| Parts of Speech | Function/ Meanings | Examples www.englishfn.com |
|---|---|---|
| 1. Noun | Name of a Person, Place, thing or idea | Amy, Maria, Books, Pen, Shop, Fairness, Keyboard, Mobile etc. |
| 2. Pronoun | Replace the name of a Person, Place, thing | He, She, We, Us, I, They, It, Our, Their, This, That, You, Me, Her, Him |
| 3. Verb | Express an action or state of being | Go, Ask, Jump, Think, Want, Eat, Run, is, am, are, was, were, |
| 4. Adverb | Describes verb, adjective or adverb | Silently, Quickly, Before, Slowly, Always, Soon, |
| 5. Preposition | Describes Place, time or direction | About, into, during, on, to, Through, After, across, |
| 6. Adjective | Modifies noun or pronoun | Small, big, Black, well |
| 7. Conjunction | Join words, phrases | For, And, Nor, But, Or, Yet, So |
| 8. Interjection | Express strong emitions | Oh!, hey!, Hurrah!, Wow! |

*EnglishFN*
*https://www.englishfn.com/8-parts-of-speech/*

## What does the word critical mean?

The word "critical"' comes from the Latin word "criticus," which means a judge, an assessor, or an estimator. It also refers to a grammarian who identifies false or spurious passages in a literary work.[1] Critical thinking itself comprises various skill sets that converge to enable you to interpret and comprehend the information you're attempting to analyze. These critical thinking skills hold significant importance in various contexts, even if their importance might not be immediately apparent. Developing these skills ensures that you're equipped to handle almost any situation that demands analytical thinking and problem-solving. When you can make purposeful and reflective judgments, you'll discover that you're much more adept at dealing with whatever challenges life presents.

## Excerpt from "Thinking Critically" p. 43[2]

*It is by questioning, making sense of situations, and analyzing issues that we examine our thinking and the thinking of others these critical activities aid us in reaching the best possible conclusions and decisions. The critical is also related to the word criticize which means to question and valuate unfortunately, the ability to criticize is often used destructively, to tear down someone else's thinking. Criticism however can also be constructive-analyzing for the purpose of developing a better understanding of what is going on. Thinking is the way you make sense of the world thinking critically is thinking about your thinking so that you can clarify and improve it.*

---

1. "Critical," in *Online Etymology Dictionary*, accessed August 7, 2023, https://www.etymonline.com/search?q=critical.

2. "Thinking Critically," *Studylib.Net*, February 12, 2017, https://studylib.net/doc/18666896/thinking-critically.

## Excerpt from Critical Thinking Beginners Guide pages. 15, 19

*Define target. Critical thinking- the objective analysis and evaluation of an issue in order to form a judgment.*[3]

The key part of that definition is the need to form a judgment. Critical thinking precedes the judgment. People tend to judge before gathering all the necessary information. This mode of thinking is habitual and unproductive.

### What does "belief" mean in etymology?

The meaning of "conviction of the truth of a proposition or alleged fact without knowledge" dates back to the 1530s. It is also "sometimes used to include the absolute conviction or certainty which accompanies knowledge."[4] This is where many of our people enter a state of programmed denial, incorrectly and harmfully merging beliefs with knowledge.

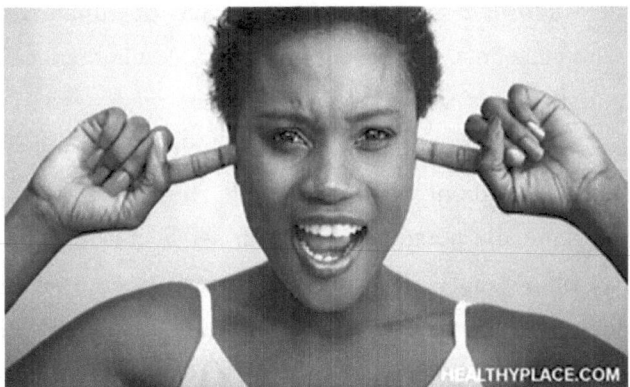

Source: Healthyplace.com

---

3. Carl Patterson, *Critical Thinking Beginner's Guide: Learn How Reasoning by Logic Improves Effective Problem Solving. The Tools to Think Smarter, Level Up Intuition to Reach Your Potential and Grow Your Mindfulness*, 2020, 15, 19.

4. *Belief*, n.d., *The Century Dictionary*, n.d., http://triggs.djvu.org/century-dictionary.com/djvu2jpgframes.php?volno=01&page=0513&query=belief.

## What is knowledge?

From the late 14th century, "knowledge" referred to the "capacity for knowing, understanding; familiarity." It also denoted the "fact or condition of knowing; awareness of a fact," as well as "news, notice, information, learning," or an organized body of facts or teachings.[5] One of the biggest obstacles preventing people from embracing critical thinking is denial.

## Excerpt from "Disinformation and You"

*The refusal to look at facts and evidence to the contrary of what we've already buckled down to accept as reality, usually dependent upon our political, religious, and cultural leaning. If a new narrative doesn't fit our chosen one, we find many creative ways to reject it even if it is truer and more accurate than what we are choosing to believe.*[6]

Denial is the most challenging barrier to overcome when we encounter information that challenges and potentially shatters our deeply rooted beliefs. Such a significant and fundamental disruption of our foundation, our core, by new information might lead to a change of perspective, and even worse, force us to admit we were mistaken. There are some things about which we'd prefer to be mistaken. Faced with material that could potentially alter our sense of self, we tend to close ourselves off or deny it. At times, we struggle to process it fully. Once individuals have formed their worldview and self-identity, it becomes extremely difficult to change their perspectives. Even presenting them with indisputable facts will seldom influence them.

According to Simply Psychology, "Cognitive dissonance refers to a situation involving conflicting attitudes, beliefs, or behaviors. This produces a feeling of mental discomfort leading to an alteration in

---

5. "Knowledge," in *Online Etymology Dictionary*, accessed July 2, 2023, https://www.etymonline.com/search?q=knowledge.

6. Marie D. Jones, *Disinformation and You: Identify Propaganda and Manipulation* (Canton, MI, United States of America: Visible Ink Press, 2021).

one of the attitudes, beliefs, or behaviors to reduce the discomfort and restore balance."[7]

### John 1:1

*"In beginning was the word, and the word was with God, and the word was God."*

An interesting dynamic emerges when individuals fervently support the Bible, but seem to overlook or avoid discussing this particular scripture. Simply put, the words that we speak have a paramount significance to universal principles: Love, Truth, Peace, Freedom, Justice.

### Matthew 6:33

*"Seek ye first the kingdom of heaven and all these things would be added unto you."*

### Exodus 20:12; HKMHTS Chpt. XLVII: Ver.9[8]

*"Honor thy Father and thy Mother, that thy days may be long upon the Earth land which the Lord thy God Allah hath given thee."*

## A Divine Warning by the Prophet for The Nations

The citizens of all free national governments according to their national constitution are all of one family bearing one free national name. Those who fails to recognize the free national name of their constitonal government are classed as undesireables, and are subject to all inferior names and abuses and mistreatments that the citizens care to bestow upon them. It is a sin for any group of people to violate the national constitutional laws of a free national government and cling

---

7. "Cognitive Dissonance Theory," Simply Psychology, accessed July 2, 2023, https://www.simplypsychology.org/cognitive-dissonance.html.

8. Noble Prophet Drew Ali, The Holy Koran of the Moorish Holy Temple of Science - Circle 7: Re-Print of Original 1926 Publication (Califa Media Publishing, 2014).

to the names and the principles that delude to slavery.

I, the Prophet, was prepared by the Great God Allah to warn my people to repent from their sinful ways and go back to that state of mind to their foremothers' Divine and National principles that they will be law–abiders and receive their right as citizens, according to the free national constitution that was prepared for all free national beings. They are to claim their own free national name and religion. There is but one issue for them to be recognized by this government and of the earth and it comes only through the connection of the Moorish Divine National Movement, which is incorporated in this government and recognized by all other nations of the world. And truly they and their children can receive their divine rights, unmolested by other citizens that they can cast a free national ballot at the polls under the free national constitution of the States government and not under a granted privilege, as has been the existing condition for many generations.

> **Moor** (mūˑɹ, mōˑɹ), *sb.*² Forms: 4 **Maur**, 4–7 **More**, 5 **Moure, Mowre**, 6, 8 **Maure**, 6–7 **Moore**, 7– **Moor**. (Now with initial capital.) [ME. *More*, a. F. *More* (13th c.), *Maure*, ad. L. *Maurus* (med. L. *Mōrus*), Gr. Μαῦρος. Cf. Sp., Pg., It. *Moro*; MDu. *Moor, Moer* (Du. *Moor*), OHG. *Mŏr*, pl. *Mŏri* (MHG. *Mŏr, Mar,* mod.G. *Mohr*).
> The L. *Maurus*, Gr. Μαῦρος may possibly be from some ancient North African language. Some believe the word to be merely a use of Gr. μαυρός black (which on this view is aphetic from ἀμαυρός blind); but this adj. (or at least this sense of it) is confined to late Gr., and may even be derived from the ethnic name.]
> **1.** In *Ancient History*, a native of *Mauretania*, a region of Northern Africa corresponding to parts of Morocco and Algeria. In later times, one belonging to the people of mixed Berber and Arab race, Mohammedan in religion, who constitute the bulk of the population of North-western Africa, and who in the 8th c. conquered Spain. In the Middle Ages, and as late as the 17th c., the Moors were commonly supposed to be mostly black or very swarthy (though the existence of 'white Moors' was recognized), and hence the word was often used for 'negro'; cf. BLACKAMOOR.

Legal definition of Moor, Black's Law Dictionary 4th Deluxe Edition,1951
Source: DrAlimElBey.com

You who doubt whether I, the Prophet, and my principles are right for the redemption for my people go to those that know law in the City Hall and among the officials in your government and asked them under an intelligent tone, and they will be glad to render you a favorable reply, for they are glad to see me bring you out of darkness into light.

Money doesn't make the man; It is free national standards and power that makes a man and a nation. The wealth of all national governments, gold and silver and commerce belong to the citizens alone and without your national citizenship by name and principles, you have no true wealth, and I am hereby calling all true citizens that stand for a national free government, and the enforcement of the constitution to help me and my great missionary work because I need all support from all true American citizens of the United States of America help me to save my people who have fallen from the constitutional laws of the government. I am depending on your support to get them back to the constitutional fold again that they will learn to love instead of hate, and will live according to Love, Truth Peace, Freedom and Justice supporting our free national constitution of the United States of America.

I love my people and I desire their unity and mine back to their own free National and Divine standard because day by day they have been violating the national and constitutional laws of their government by claiming names and principles that are unconstitutional. If Italians, Greeks, English, Chinese, Japanese, Turks, and Arabians are forced to proclaim their free national name and religion before the constitutional government of the United States of America, it is no more than right that the law should be enforced upon all American citizens alike. In all other governments when a man is born and raised there and asked for his national descent name and he fails to give it, he is misused, imprisoned, or exiled. Any group of people that failed to answer up to the constitutional standards of law by name and principles, because to be a citizen of any government you must claim your national descent name. Because they placed their trust upon issue and names formed by their forefathers.

The word Negro deludes in the Latin language to the word; The same as the word "colored" deludes that is painted, varnished and dyed. And every nation must bear a national descent name of their forefathers, because honoring thy fathers and thy mothers your days will be lengthened upon this earth these names have never been recognized by any true American citizens of this day. Through your free national name you are known and recognized by all nations of the earth that are recognized by said national government in which they live.

The 14th and 15th amendments brought the North and South in unit, placing the southerners who were at the time without power, with the constitutional body of power. And at the time, 1865, the free national constitutional law that was enforced since 1774 declared all men equal and free, and if all men are declared by the free national constitution to be free and equal since that constitution has never been changed, there is no need for the application of the 14th or 15th amendments for the salvation of our people and citizens.

"The Great Meeting Is On!"
Source: Koran Questions for Moorish Americans, Moorish Guide Publishing Company Chicago, c. 1928

So, there is but one supreme issue for my people to use to redeem that which was lost, and that is through the above statements. Then the lion and lamb can lie down together in yonder hills. And neither will be harmed, because Love, Truth, Peace, Freedom, and Justice will be reigning in this land. In those days the United States will be one of the greatest civilized and prosperous governments of the world. But if the above principles are not carried out by the citizens and my people in this government, the worst is yet to come because the Great God of the universe is not pleased with the works that are being performed in North America by my people and this great sin must be removed from the land to save it from enormous earthquakes disease etc, and I, the Prophet do hereby believe that this administration of the government being more wisely prepared by more genius citizens that believe in their free national constitution and laws and through the help of such classes of citizens, I, the Prophet, truly believe that my people will find the true and divine way of their forefathers, and learn to stop serving carnal customs and merely ideas of man, that have never done them any good but I have always harmed them.

So, I, the Prophet, am hereby calling aloud with a divine plea to all true American citizens to help me to remove this great sin which has been committed and is being practiced by my people in the United States of America. Because they know it is not the true and divine way and, without understanding they have fallen from the true light into utter darkness of sin and there is not a nation on earth today that will recognize them socially, religiously, politically or economically, etc. and their present condition of their endearment in which they themselves try to force upon a civilized world. They will not refrain from their sinful ways of action and their deeds have brought segregation, and everything that brings harm to human beings on earth. And they fought the Southern for all these great misuses, but I have traveled in the South and have examined conditions there, and it is the works of my people continuously practicing the things which bring dishonor, disgrace, and disrespect to any nation that lives the life. And I am hereby calling on all true American citizens for moral support and finance to help me and my great missionary work to bring my people out of darkness into marvelous light.

# End Notes

Ali, Noble Prophet Drew. *The Holy Koran of the Moorish Holy Temple of Science - Circle 7: Re-Print of Original 1926 Publication*. Califa Media Publishing, 2014.

*Belief*. n.d. The Century Dictionary. http://triggs.djvu.org/century-dictionary.com/djvu2jpgframes.php?volno=01&page=0513&query=belief.

Simply Psychology. "Cognitive Dissonance Theory." Accessed July 2, 2023. https://www.simplypsychology.org/cognitive-dissonance.html.

"Critical." In *Online Etymology Dictionary*. Accessed August 7, 2023. https://www.etymonline.com/search?q=critical.

Jones, Marie D. *Disinformation and You: Identify Propaganda and Manipulation*. Canton, MI, United States of America: Visible Ink Press, 2021.

"Knowledge." In *Online Etymology Dictionary*. Accessed July 2, 2023. https://www.etymonline.com/search?q=knowledge.

Patterson, Carl. *Critical Thinking Beginner's Guide: Learn How Reasoning by Logic Improves Effective Problem Solving. The Tools to Think Smarter, Level Up Intuition to Reach Your Potential and Grow Your Mindfulness*, 2020.

"Thinking Critically." *Studylib.Net*, February 12, 2017. https://studylib.net/doc/18666896/thinking-critically.

# Chapter 2

## Man Know Thyself

Contrary to popular belief there are 5 true universal components which equally make up the natural man and woman as opposed to the legal term artificial persons. So-called persons of color, Indian, Native American, Pan-African, black, negro etc., are all 3/5 colorable brands placed on Moorish indigenous peoples to confuse and trick them out of their lands, resources, nationality, inheritance, culture—the list goes on.

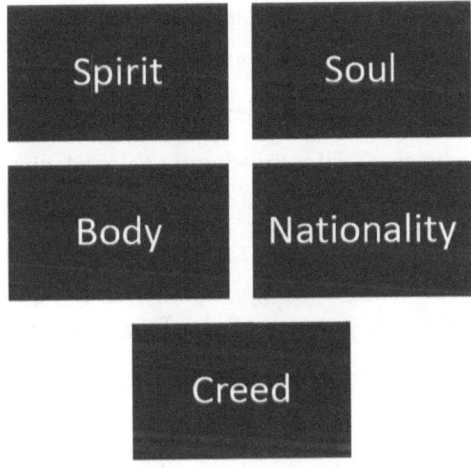

1. SPIRIT - the indestructible God essence in man.

2. SOUL - actions of the mind's powers (Thinking, Reasoning, Willing, & Understanding).

3. BODY - flesh, human vehicle made of the earth; (often indigenous to the land of birth).

4. NATIONALITY- the descendant birth attachment though and the special nation or tribe; Free National Name, Lineage identity.

5. CREED - religious path of God consciousness established through forefathers' vine and fig tree.

According to the Circle 7 divinely prepared by the Prophet Noble Drew Ali:

> *16. Through sin and disobedience every nation has suffered slavery, due to the fact that they honored not the creed and principles of their forefathers.*
>
> *17. That is why the nationality of the Moors was taken away from them in 1774 and the word negro, black and colored, was given to the Asiatics of America who were of Moorish descent because they honor not the principles of their mother and father and straight after the gods of Europe of whom they knew nothing.[1]*

Noble Drew Ali was aware of the importance of nationality and birth rights. This can be cross referenced and analyzed with an examination of Chapter 47:

### Chapter XLVII
### Egypt, the Capital Empire of the Dominion of Africa

1. The inhabitants of Africa are the descendants of the ancient Canaanites from the land of Canaan.
2. Old man Cush and his family are the first inhabitants of Africa who came from the land of Canaan.
3. His father Ham and his family were second. Then came the word Ethiopia, which means the demarcation line of the dominion of Amexem, the first true and divine name of Africa. The dividing of the land between the father and the son.
4. The dominion of Cush, North-East and South-East Africa and North-West and South-West was his father's dominion of Africa.
5. In later years many of their bretheren from Asia and the Holy Lands joined them.

---

1. Timothy Drew Ali, *The Holy Koran of the Moorish Holy Temple of Science - Circle 7: Re-Print of Original 1926 Publication* (Califa Media Publishing, 2014), chap. XLVII.

6. The Moabites from the land of Moab who received permission from the Pharaohs of Egypt to settle and inhabit North-West Africa; they were the founders and are the true possessors of the present Moroccan Empire. With their Canaanite, Hittite, and Amorite bretheren who sojourned from the land of Canaan seeking new homes.

7. Their dominion and inhabitation extended from North-East and South-West Africa, across great Atlantis even unto the present North, South, and Central America and also Mexico and the Atlantis Islands; before the great earthquake, which caused the great Atlantic Ocean.

8. The River Nile was dredged and made by the ancient Pharaohs of Egypt, in order to trade with the surrounding kingdoms. Also the Niger river was dredged by the great Pharaoh of Egypt in those ancient days for trade, and it extends eastward from the River Nile, westward across the great Atlantic. It was used for trade and transportation.

9. According to all true and divine records of the human race there is no negro, black, or colored race attached to the human family, because all the inhabitants of Africa were and are of the human race, descendants of the ancient Canaanite nation from the holy land of Canaan.

10. What your ancient forefathers were, you are today without doubt or contradiction.

11. There is no one who is able to change man from the descendant nature of his forefathers; unless his power extends beyond the great universal Creator Allah Himself.

12. These holy and divine laws are from the Prophet, Noble Drew Ali, the founder of the uniting of the Moorish Science Temple of America.

13. These laws are to be strictly preserved by the members of all the Temples, of the Moorish Science Temple of America. That they will learn to open their meeting and guide it according to the principles of Love, Truth, Peace, Freedom and Justice.
14. Every subordinate Temple of the Grand-Major Temple is to form under the covenant of Love, Truth, Peace, Freedom and Justice; and to create their own laws and customs, in conjunction with the laws of the Holy Prophet and the Grand Temple. I, the Prophet, Noble Drew Ali, was sent by the great God, Allah, to warn all Asiatics of America to repent from their sinful ways; before that great and awful day that is sure to come.
15. The time has come when every nation must worship under its own vine and fig tree, and every tongue must confess his own.[2]

A lot of misconceptions are due to the intentional miseducation of indigenous people by the school systems. From grammar school, middle school, high school even into college, silent weapons for quiet wars have been put in place. One way to hide something is to put it in plain sight, then overload the potentially interested with tons of distractions, beliefs, entertainment etc. to keep them in a state of mind of confusion and ignorance.

> "To turn people into slaves, ye must first teach them they were slaves, came from slaves over and over until their offspring become volunteer slaves." Da 13th Sun.[3]

---

2. Drew Ali, *Holy Koran Circle 7*
3. Mishaal Talib Mahfuz El Bey, *The Torch: A Guide to S.E.L.F.* (Califa Media Publishing, 2020).

Moors possess an ancient nationality and birthright that ties them to geographical landmasses, territories, populations, lands, monuments, languages, and so forth. Individuals who lack an understanding of Moorish history, which is essentially WORLD HISTORY, often make statements like:

*"If our people were Moors then where is Moorland?"*

*"Moor and black mean the same thing".*

*"The Moors were traitors and sold out to the white men."*

*"If the Moors were so great, how did they fall"?*

Let's put these under the microscope...

## LAND Definition & Legal Meaning

Definition & Citations:

*...in the most general sense, comprehends any ground, soil, or earth whatsoever, as meadows, pastures, woods, moors, waters, marshes, furzes, and heath. Co. Litt 4a. The word "land" includes not only the soil, but everything attached to it, whether attached by the course of nature, as trees, herbage, and water, or by the hand of man, as buildings and fences. Mott v. Palmer, 1 N. Y. 572; Nessler v. Neher, 18 Neb. 649, 26 N. W. 471; Higgins Fuel Co. v. Snow, 113 Fed. 433, 51 C. C. A. 267; Lightfoot v. Grove, 5 Heisk. (Tenn.) 477; Johnson v. Richardson, 33 Miss. 464; Mitchell v. Warner, 5 Conn. 517; Myers v. League, 62 Fed. 659, 10 C. C. A. 571. 2 Bl. Comm. 16, 17. Land is the solid material of the earth, whatever may be the ingredients of which it is composed, whether soil, rock, or other substance. Civ. Code Cal.*[4]

As you can see, the entire planet constitutes Moorish lands. What stands out is the presence of the word "Moor" in a law dictionary,

---

4. Henry C. Black, "Land," in *Black's Law Dictionary* (St. Paul, MN: West Publishing, 1951).

"There is now however a bigger issue at stake and that is the destruction of the Moorish nation which was known as societies Republicae Ea Al Maurikanos which translated as the al Moroccan Republic society. At the time of the founding of this country, America was called al Moroccan because it was part of the Moroccan empire known as a maxim. It was transliterated into America by the colonists and eventually a story was made-up that America was named after Amerigo Vespucci, navigator any history teacher I ever had who mentioned Vespucci always commented how it made no sense to name America after a seemingly insignificant navigator. We now realized that there was a significant motive to hide the history of what had transpired.

What is most significant, however, is that the mores are hardwired into the entire schematic of the Holy Land in such a way that, ultimately, they cannot be ignored. Though virtually none of our major world politicians could admit it, the Moors are not only a part of the infrastructure of Jerusalem but of the entire world and its political structure. The Morris issue was like a secret code but it is not one they really use they of course know about it and mimic it with some of their secret symbols in an attempt to siphon off the power they would never actually use this Morse code itself because it is tantamount to making their House of cars fall down. You see, this Moorish code I am referring to is another word for revelation, but I am not talking about a canned stereotype version of revelation that you might hear a so-called religious zealot talk about. Exposing this Moorish code reveals the truth, and the truth leads to more and more revelation of the way things really are. It is more like a tsunami wave that is about to hit our entire our culture. It may be far off on the horizon right now but it is just a matter of time before it hits the shore there are a lot of things to Reconcile, but I am not referring to slave reparations the injustice of slavery is really just the tip of the iceberg the issues are far beyond human slavery if everyone, not just the so-called black people, are going to find their way back home they need to know the truth."

---

5. Peter Moon, *The Montauk Book of the Dead* (New York: Sky Books, 2005).

precisely defining the dominions of Moorish peoples, both past and enduring. The Americas represent the true old world, not the "new world" as various fraudulent narratives have falsely suggested about figures like Amerigo Vespucci, Christopher Columbus, and other mixed European backgrounds. Moors have had a presence in the Americas since ancient times.

The 1828 Noah Webster Dictionary defines the word America as AMER'ICA, noun (from Amerigo Vespucci, a Florentine, credited with the first European discovery of the western continent).

**Noah Webster Dictionary 1828 Edition**
- American
- AMER'ICAN, *adjective* Pertaining to America.
- AMER'ICAN, *noun* A native of America; <u>originally</u> applied to the aboriginals, or copper-colored races, found here by the Europeans; but now applied to the descendants of Europeans born in America.
- The name *American* must always exalt the pride of patriotism. – *Washington*
- http://webstersdictionary1828.com/Dictionary/Americ

*WebstersDictionay1828.c0m/Dictionary/American*

The true Americans are the various copper complexion people of the lands. The Moorish descendants have been miseducated to disassociate themselves mentally from the Americas thereby abandoning their birth right and inheritance.

### Excerpt from "America As A Land Of Opportunity"
### Subject: Why Increase the sons of Africa in America

> "Why should the Palatine Moors/Germans be suffered to swarm into our Pennsylvania settlements... they will never adopt our customs any more than they can adopt our complexion (White Skin). All of Africa, Asia, and America (except) for us are black. Russia, Italy, Spain, France, Swedes and the Germans are black! All of Africa is tawny (black) Asia chiefly tawny (black) America exclusive of the newcomers, wholly so. In Europe the Spaniards, French, Italians, Russians, and Swedes are generally of what we call a swarthy (black) complexion. So are the Germans also."[6]

---

6. Benjamin Franklin, America as a Land of Opportunity, Digital History, 1751, accessed August 20, 2023, https://www.digitalhistory.uh.edu/disp_textbook_print.cfm?smtid=3&psid=85.

Time out—lets pull some book references...

- James H. Anderson, *Riddles of Prehistoric Times*
  "The little black Welsh/Brits settled in Scotland, France, Spain, British Isles and all over Europe." [7]

- "Our Remote Ancestry : Winchell, Alexander , September 1, 1884, secs. 1818–1900.[8]

- Roman Historian Tacitus and the Origins of the Black Britons, The Anthropological Review, Vol. 8 by Anthropological Society of London, London: Asher & Co., 1870, pg. 202

- "The Iberians Are Black People," Ivan Van Sertima, *African Presence in Early Europe*.[9]

- Joseph Ritson ESQ, Anals Of Caledonian Picts and Scots, vol. 2, pp 7, 27.[10]

  "The Brits look like the Ethiopian."

  "The picts are brown skinned with curly hair"

- Dr. Thurman NATURE JOURNAL OF SCIENCE pg. 92

  "From the evidence at hand it appears that the Iberians occupied the whole of western Europe at one time."

Can somebody say receipts?

Now, when someone asks you where are the Moorish lands, you can legitimately say: You're standing on them.

---

7. James H. Anderson, *Riddles of Prehistoric Times* (Alpha Edition, 2019).

8. "Our Remote Ancestry," in *Internet Archive*, September 1, 1884, accessed June 3, 2023, https://archive.org/details/jstor-25118417.

9. Ivan Van Sertima, African Presence in Early Europe (Transaction Publishers, 1985).

10. Joseph Ritson ESQ, Anals Of Caledonian Picts and Scots, vol. 2 (London: Pall Mall, 1828).

## What's in a Name?

Moorish people have been influenced by internal betrayals, media, and shadowy forces—some knowingly, others unknowingly—to believe that the label they give themselves holds no real significance or impact on how they are perceived and treated. This couldn't be further from the truth. A name establishes the bedrock of your identity: your origin, heritage, culture, language, and more. In legal terms, this is known as your status.

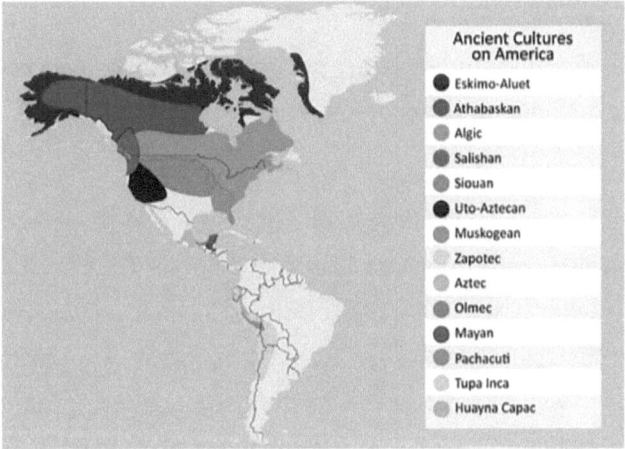

*Ancient Cultures in the Americas*
*Source: Miguel Angel / Vectezy.com.*

To address any problem, it must first be identified at its root. So-called black organizations have consistently and reliably failed to address these roots; instead, they focus on symptoms. This is why we repeatedly encounter redundant and unproductive outcomes. There is a great deal of marching, financial resources being spent, grief, and misery. One of the primary keys, and the initial step towards resolving the issues faced by so-called black people, is recognizing the root cause.

*"If you don't do anything else declare a nationality."* – Noble Drew Ali

The term "black," when used to refer to oneself, must be eradicated from the minds of Moorish people for any meaningful change to occur. As a person thinks, so they become. Manipulating the status of the aboriginal and indigenous people was one of the primary tactics employed. Recall the scene in "The Matrix" where Morpheus informed Neo that he was a slave? The prison Morpheus spoke of was Mental Slavery: intangible, yet it profoundly impacts so-called colored individuals in every aspect of their lives.

The reader might be asking:

*When did this mental slavery start with so called black people, and how has this infamous word "black" come into play?*

The semantic evolution of "black" took a turn to denote "having malignant or deadly purposes," and even came to be associated with death, giving rise to phrases like "black curse" (1583), and harking back to earlier times, "The Black Death." The term "blac" underwent a final transformation when a "K" was appended to it, creating a new derogatory way to refer to the Moors (who are today referred to as so-called Blacks). This group had inhabited Europe for thousands of years but was now subjected to hatred and persecution. They were labeled the Queen's Black enemies, the blackamoors, and eventually just reduced to the adjective used as a noun: "blacks".

It should be noted for the record that the term used to describe the color black in historical and classical Europe was the word "Moor" (also "Melas"). The original Greeks in Europe referred to themselves as Moors, spelling it "Mauros." Variants of this term are found in every European language, albeit with different spellings. Thus, you have "Mohr" in German, "Maure" and "Mire" in French, "Moor" in English, "Moros" in Italian and Spanish, and "Mor" in Old and Middle English. All these variants conveyed the same meaning: the color/class/ caste now known as black.

The Europeans took away our names, labeling us niggers, colored, blacks, negros, Africans, sub Saharans, etc. All of these are derogatory terms. We are none of those. Not Jamaicans, not Nigerians, nor Americans. We are Moors, a people tracing back to the most ancient times. Umoros, Umorus, Muurs, Mawus — the children of light, the bearers of civilization and compassion, the golden ones, the first people, Ethiopians, Mauritanians, and Mauritians.

When you check ancient history, you'll come across accounts of the Moors, but you won't find mention of "negros." The pale ones (the blanks) appropriated our names and falsely claimed it only referred to Arab Muslims' conquest of Spain. No! The Greeks were familiar with the Muurs, as were the Romans, the ancient Hindu (Indians), and the Chinese. This is because the ancient Egyptians referred to their land as Ta-Meri or Ta-Muri, the land of the Muurs. They were seafarers who navigated the globe and brought enlightenment to all. We are those Muurs. We are their descendants. We are not "the blacks." The "blancho" people, today's so-called white people, they are "the blaccas."

## Excerpt: The Origin of the Word 'Black': How Black Entered the English Language

*The following source traces the history of the term black. The Old English blac was used, like blanc, to refer to a fair person, someone "devoid of colour". It was only in the 16th century that we saw the semantic change of blac to refer to something dark (night-colour): The*
https://thirdhour.org/

word 'Black' can be traced back to its proto Indo-European origins through the word 'blac' which meant pale, wan, colourless, or albino. 'Blac' was incorporated into Old French as Blanc, Italian and Spanish as Blanco, Bianca, Bianco, Bianchi.

*In Old English "blac" person meant fair; someone devoid of colour, similar to the word "blanc" which still means white or fair person. In Middle English the word was spelt as "blaec" same thing as the modern word "black", only at that time, around 1051 AD, it still meant a fair skin, or so-called white person. The words "blacca" an Old/Middle English word still resonates with "blanke" the Dutch-Germanic term for white people of today. It was not till the sixteenth century that the semantic broadening of black occured- both figurative connotations as well as literal.* [11]

So as you can see the word black actually means PALE.

From terms like "blac," "blake," "bleaken," "blaccen," which literally meant "to bleach out or make white, blond or pale," emerged the figurative meanings "to stain someone"s reputation," "defame," or "darken." Essentially, by this time, "blac" had come to signify a night-like color, something dark. One could say it was a very dramatic shift indeed. This era also witnessed the Vandals and the Goths actively inscribing themselves into history, while simultaneously erasing European Mauros (melan-chros or melanin people) from it.[12]

In the latter part of the 17th century, the meaning of "Moor" began to evolve, shifting from simply "black" or "non-white" to encompass "Muslim non-white," which also included Muslims from the East Indies. The term "Schwart" started to be employed more broadly to refer to non-whites, encompassing a majority of peoples ranging from

---

11. "The Origin of the Word 'Black': How Black Entered the English Language," Suite101.com, accessed August 22, 2023, http://suite101.com/article/the-origin-of-the-word-black-a50079#ixzz1wJ950Gey.

12. Don Jaide, "Etymology of Black and Moor – Oguejiofo Annu | Rasta Livewire," June 4, 2012, https://www.africaresource.com/rasta/sesostris-the-great-the-egyptian-hercules/etymology-of-black-and-moor-oguejiofo-annu/comment-page-1/.

India through Indonesia, and at times, Africans and occasionally Americans.

Both "Moor" and "Moren" had also been used to denote Americans (in Antwerp, 1563, and Brazil, 1550s, 1640s), indicating a pattern where both "Moor" and "Swart" were adaptable enough to cover a wide spectrum of brown to dark brown individuals. A 1691 English-Dutch dictionary defines "Moor" as "Moor"; "a black Moor" as "een Zwarte", and "Tawny Moor" as "een Gele Moor", demonstrating how the English term "tawny" was applied, often to Americans.

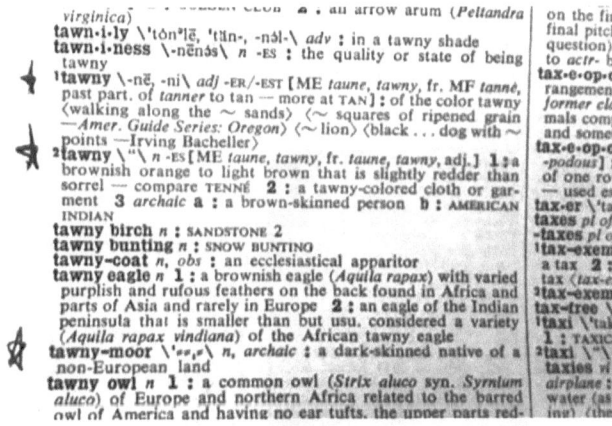

A 1718 Portuguese-Dutch dictionary provides insight into color connotations. Portuguese "pardo" (applied to Americans) is equated with Dutch "Donkerverwig" and "swart". "Moor" and "caffir/kaffir" are considered equivalent, and "Mooreland" is still used to refer to the "land of blacks". As the 18th century progressed, "zwart" began to replace "Moor" in Dutch dictionaries. However, a change can be observed in the 1771 dictionary, where the author also employs the term "neger"

In 1783, a French-Dutch dictionary states: "Moor – inhabitant of the; Mauritania = Moor, Negro, Black, Moorish, See Maure; Maure = Black, who is in service to some lord = Moorish Moor or Moors = Inhabitants of Mauritania = Moors, inhabitants of Moorland, Blacks,

Negroes. Black = Black."

Between 1844 and 1845, Dutch dictionaries shifted the meaning of Moor to refer specifically to a North African. By 1913, "Moor" was not in common use, as compared to "neger" or "zwart". It was also noted that by 1845, "neger" had replaced the term "negro" in the 18th century. "By European peoples, the so-called negroes became especially known as slaves in the colonies; from that, the word so-called negro also became a very common term in our language." This association of "neger" with slave was thus clearly established in the Dutch language. Several other Dutch-French and Dutch-English dictionaries also list "slave" as one of the meanings of "negre", "negro maure", and "zwart"..

A 1607 dictionary defines "moreno" as "brun, noir, obscure, couleur d"olives", indicating quite a range of colors. In any case, it"s evident that the "Mauri-Moor" group of terms in various languages did not exclusively refer to absolute black or blackish alone, but could indeed encompass a range of darker skin tones. This is also true for "nigri" (Italian for "dark-skinned person") and its variations. The term "aubnigros" next to "nigros" clearly indicates a variation, while "preto" (black) encompasses all of the mentioned colors: copperish or reddish, and so on.

An Irish Gaelic saga from the tenth century AD (reprinted in 1643) recounts that Danish-Irish raiders attacked Spain and Mauritania in the ninth century AD. They carried off a great host of captives from

Spain to Erin, and these are known as the Blue Men of Erin, for "Mauri" is the same as black man, and "Mauritania" is the same as blackness. "...long indeed were the Blue men in Erin"; the Gaelic text uses "Mauri" and "negri", and "Mauritania" and "negritudo", evidently borrowed from Latin (the concept of "blue men" is described in the original Gaelic words).

From this, we can see how the interchange of the term "Mori" for "negro" spread to northern Europe. Simultaneously, we can see how both words could be used for shades of brown, since from our modern perspective, the Mauritanians (Berbers, Moors, etc.) are not considered to have black or blue skin tones. It's possible, of course, that they have lightened due to mixing with Romans, Spaniards, Arabs, Vandals, and so on, but some of that change in color could have occurred prior to the ninth century.[13]

---

13. Jack D. Forbes, *Africans and Native Americans: The Language of Race and the Evolution of Red-Black Peoples* (Chicago: University of Illinois Press, 1993).

# End Notes

Anderson, James H. *Riddles of Prehistoric Times*. Alpha Edition, 2019.

Black, Henry C. "Land." In *Black's Law Dictionary*. West Publishing, 1951.

Black, Henry Campbell. "Person." In *Black's Law Dictionary*. Springer, May 31, 1992.

Chang, Pao. *Word Magic: The Powers and Occult Definitions of Words* (Second Edition). Esoteric Knowledge Publishing, 2019.

Forbes, Jack D. *Africans and Native Americans: The Language of Race and the Evolution of Red-Black Peoples*. Chicago: University of Illinois Press, 1993.

Franklin, Benjamin. *America as a Land of Opportunity. Digital History*, 1751. Accessed August 20, 2023. https://www.digitalhistory.uh.edu/disp_textbook_print.cfm?smtid=3&psid=85.

Jaide, Don. "Etymology of Black and Moor – Oguejiofo Annu | Rasta Livewire," June 4, 2012. https://www.africaresource.com/rasta/sesostris-the-great-the-egyptian-hercules/etymology-of-black-and-moor-oguejiofo-annu/comment-page-1/.

Mahfuz El Bey, Mishaal Talib. *The Torch: A Guide to S.E.L.F.* Califa Media Publishing, 2020.

Moon, Peter. *The Montauk Book of the Dead*. New York: Sky Books, 2005.

Noble Drew Ali, Timothy. *The Holy Koran of the Moorish Holy Temple of Science - Circle 7: Re-Print of Original 1926 Publication*. Califa Media Publishing, 2014. chap. XLVII.

"Our Remote Ancestry." In *Internet Archive*, September 1, 1884. Accessed June 3, 2023. https://archive.org/details/jstor-25118417.

Ritson, Joseph, ESQ. *Anals Of Caledonian Picts and Scots*. Vol. 2. London: Pall Mall, 1828.

Saggigga. "Black Presence in the Ancient British Isles." Sag-gig-ga (the Black-headed People), October 15, 2010. https://saggigga.wordpress.com/2010/10/15/blackpresenceintheancientbritishisles/.

Suite101.com. "The Origin of the Word 'Black': How Black Entered the English Language." Accessed August 22, 2023. http://suite101.com/article/the-origin-of-the-word-black-a50079#ixzz1wJ950Gey.

Van Sertima, Ivan. *African Presence in Early Europe*. Transaction Publishers, 1985.

# Chapter 3

## AbraKaDaBra

When spoken aloud, words undergo a transformation into sound, frequency, and vibration, which constitute some of the fundamental building blocks of matter. The physical world we inhabit is composed of matter; therefore, it is also composed of sound frequency and vibration. On a deeper level, the material world was brought into existence through the power of spoken words. A spoken word possesses sound, frequency, and vibration, granting it the ability to influence how energy materializes into physical form. Hence, the biblical adage, "In the beginning was the word."

The language system, which employs symbols, signs, and sounds to convey thoughts and emotions, is constructed from words. Words hold magical potency and can be either empowering or disempowering, enlightening or deceiving. One reason words can be deceptive is due to their potential for misinterpretation and misunderstanding. Moreover, the letters within a word can be rearranged to obscure its deeper meaning. Additionally, a word may have multiple definitions, which can be used by judges and attorneys to manipulate you into temporarily relinquishing your natural, God-given rights. This underscores the importance of learning how to decode words and paying close attention to their definitions.

It's worth noting that one etymological root of the word "language" is the Latin term "lingua," meaning tongue. When we dissect the word "language" into its constituent parts, we get "lan," "gu," and "age."

### Language = Lan/ Gu/ Age

"Lan" is the feminine name for orchid in Chinese and Vietnamese. In Vietnamese, "lan" also signifies "unicorn" when considering the context and masking, originating from the term "Ky lan." When we translate "Ky lan" from Vietnamese to Latin, we arrive at the word "unicornis." The "Ky lan" was a dragon-like creature believed to protect only the noble individuals and was also known as the "Quilin."

"Gu" is the God of War in Dahomey mythology. Therefore, we have "Lan," a creature that safeguards the noble ones, and "Gu," the God of War. "Age" pertains to the epochs or periods within the Zodiac. Consequently, "Lan / Gu / Ages" represent the "monsters of war that protect the noble ones or golden gods" (Au-dio) throughout the ages.[1]

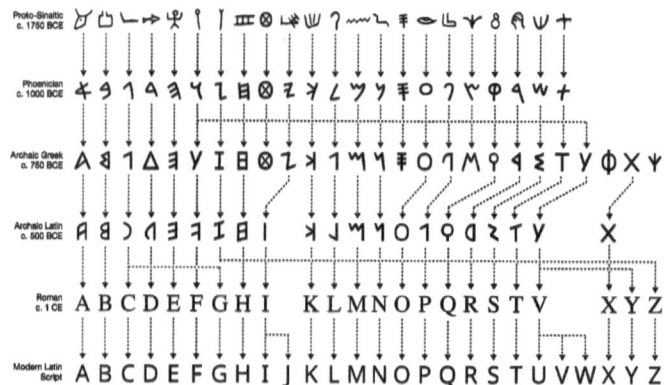

Evolution of the Alphabet
Baker (2018) https://usefulcharts.com

The assertion that Moors created all languages can be substantiated by delving into the etymology, examining symbols, signs, and grammatic scripts. Hieroglyphics transitioned into a lettering system through an upper Semitic script known as proto-Sinaitic or ancient Moabite/Canaanite, from which the Greek, Roman, Latin, and English alphabets are derived.

Ancient words transmitted through this script still retain their

---

1. Pao Chang, Word Magic: The Powers and Occult Definitions of Words (Second Edition) (Esoteric Knowledge Publishing, 2019).

inherent meaning and have been safeguarded within secret societies for centuries. This influence permeates various forms of esoteric practice and symbolism, spanning from Kabbalah to Freemasonry. The earliest manifestation of this can be traced back to the Pythagorean numeral systems employed by the Greeks, directly drawn from the ancient Moabite/Sinaitic script. This script assigned a numeric value and significance to each letter.

| àu - f | per - f | em | hru |
|--------|---------|-----|-----|
| he shall come forth | | by | day |

Excerpt from the Egytpian Book of the Dead

Remember this: when you encounter hieroglyphics or proto-Sinaitic script, it's fundamentally Moorish. Once you come to understand that everything, all along, originated from your ancient Moorish ancestors — a worldwide community — your genetic memory, imprinted in your DNA, suddenly sparks to life. Now, you have a link that

"Origins of the Roman Alphabet," Diringer (1948).

you were never informed about. The Semitic languages are, in essence, Moorish dialects. It's ludicrous to hear baseless claims, like the term "anti-Semitic," when in reality, it's the Moors who gave rise to the Semitic languages. It's time to dispel these misconceptions with concrete facts.

*Mesha Stele aka the Moabite Stone, Louvre Museum Wikipedia contributors*

*The Mesha Stele, the first major epigraphic Canaanite inscription found in the region of Palestine,[5] the longest Iron Age inscription ever found in the region, constitutes the major evidence for the Moabite language, and is a "corner-stone of Semitic epigraphy",[6] and history.[7] The stele, whose story parallels, with some differences, an episode in the Bible's Books of Kings (2 Kings 3:4–28), provides invaluable information on the Moabite language and the political relationship between Moab and Israel at one moment in the 9th century BCE.[3] It is the most extensive inscription ever recovered that refers to the kingdom of Israel (the "House of Omri");[8] it bears the earliest certain extrabiblical reference to the Israelite god Yahweh.[9][8] It is also one of four known contemporary inscriptions containing the name of Israel, the others being the Merneptah Stele, the Tel Dan Stele, and one of the Kurkh Monoliths. [10][11][12] Its authenticity has been disputed over the years, and some biblical minimalists suggest the text was not historical, but a biblical allegory. The stele itself is regarded as genuine and historical by the vast majority of biblical archaeologists today.[13]* [2]

*Mesha Stele, Louve Museum Wikipedia contributors*

To gain a deeper understanding of the ancient Moors in America, it's imperative to first delve into the intricacies of various ancient Semitic and Hamitic languages, their dialects, and the common features they share in their family character (Hieroglyphic) structures. The

---

2. "Wikiwand - Mesha Stele," Wikiwand, n.d., https://www.wikiwand.com/en/Mesha_Stele.

Semitic languages, originating from the Sons of Shem as mentioned in Genesis 10:11[3], give rise to Asshur, leading to Ashuric, Assyric, Syretic, and finally Arabic. Similarly, Aram begets Aramic, and Eber, the Son of Shelah, is integral to this Moorish heritage.

"SheM" or "Shem" denotes a name, and its root letters, SM, are the fundamental and original components of written language. They bear a connection to the Moorish-Latin term "signum" (sign or signify).

The Arabic language was prevalent among the Armenians, who are the descendants of Aaron, particularly on Saturdays in the region, which was later named Aram (Numbers 32:37-38).[4] It is from this lineage that the Aramaic language derived its name. Aram is commonly recognized to encompass tribes spanning from northern Arabia through Syria, central Mesopotamia, and up to Armenia—a name that still carries this patronymic. From there, it extended to the borders of Lydia. In the time of Homer, "Aramania" referred to Phrygia in Central Asia Minor.

During that era, the Moors residing in Syria referred to themselves as Aramaeans. These Moorish communities extended as far as Damascus in the southwest. The rule of Damascus eventually fell to Hadadezer. In a confrontation with Aram, David triumphed over twenty-two thousand (22,000) of their forces.

These dialects are the progenitors of many Semitic languages, including Ugaric, Chaldean, Syretic, Accadian, Phoenician, Moabite, Uranic, Hebrew, and Aramic. Additionally, Asshuric Arabic, Sumerian, Ghe'ez Amharic, and Farsi (Persian) can be traced back to the language of the Eloheem (Genesis 1:1).[5]

---

3. "King James Version," Bible Gateway, accessed June 3, 2023, https://www.biblegateway.com/passage/?search=Numbers+32%3A37-38&version=KJV.
4. Ibid.
5. Ibid.

The Canaanite (Moabite, Phoenician, Hebrew) Hieroglyphic Character and linguistic connection can be observed in the ancient Semitic inscriptions found on the Moabite Stone. [6]

The Hebrew term for teacher is "moreh," signifying the duty and responsibility of all those who follow the path of enlightenment. Other related terms include Ma'owr, Ma'or, M'owrah, and M'orah, all of which connote luminosity, light, and radiance within the body and spirit. [7]

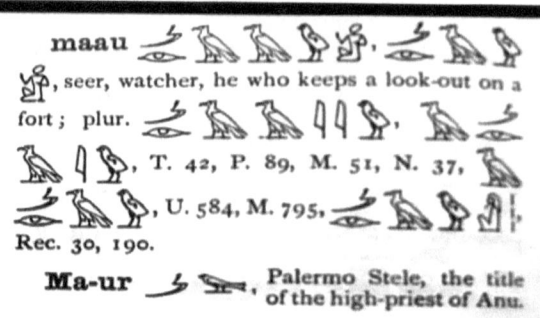

Maur Hieroglyphic from the Palermo Stele in Egypt
americaistheoldworld.com

## Koran Questions for Moorish Americans (101's & 102's)

27. Will you give in brief the line genealogy through which Yehoshua came?

**Some of the great fathers from which Yehoshua came are: Abraham, Boaz by Ruth, Jesse, King David, Solomon, Hezekiah and Joseph by Mary.**

28. Why did Allah send Yehoshua to this Earth?

**To save the Israelites from the iron hand of oppression of the pale skin nations of Europe, who were governing a portion of Palestine at that time.**

---

6. Uriel Bey and Princeps Uriel-Bai, *The Consecrated Talisman: "Salmagundi,"* 2010, 200, 202, 205, 206.

7. "Mowreh Hebrew Meaning - Old Testament Lexicon (KJV)," in *Biblestudytools.Com*, accessed July 10, 2023, https://www.biblestudytools.com/lexicons/hebrew/kjv/mowreh-2.html.

30. What was the nationality of Ruth? **Ruth was a Moabitess.**

31. What is the modern name for Moabites? **Moroccans**

32. Where is the Moroccan Empire? **Northwest Amexem**

33. What is the modern name for Amexem? **Africa** [8]

This is why Noble Drew Ali said we are Moorish Americans; we are descendants of Moroccans born in America.

In nearly every language, dialect, and culture, you'll encounter some reference to the term "Moor," whether in a positive or negative light. This acknowledges the ancient architects of civilization, drawing on the wisdom of their forebears, combined with their own knowledge. This convergence has given rise to the profound understanding that serves as the source from which the waters of eternal life flow. It is a wellspring from which all peoples have partaken, and some have tried to taint or obliterate.[9]

The Moors embody what is often referred to as "light," signifying knowledge. They serve as the guardians and originators of the fundamental principles of civilization, driving the wheels of evolution towards higher planes of consciousness. Thus, they stand as luminaries beneath the umbrella of Love, Truth, Peace, Freedom, and Justice, reflecting these values in every aspect of creation.[10]

---

8. T.S .Najee-Ullah El, ed., "Koran Questions for Moorish Americans: 101s And Additional Laws," in *Califa Uhuru: A Compilation of Literature from the Moorish Science Temple of America* (Califa Media Publishing, 2014).

9. Mishaal Talib Mahfuz El Bey, *The Torch: A Guide to S.E.L.F.* (Califa Media Publishing, 2020), 21.

10. Ibid, 21.

## The Era of the English Language

Before 1828, the Roman tribes in colonial North America spoke different Latin dialects, all of which had roots in Arabic, the language of the sophisticated Moors. In 1828, the first English dictionary was published in colonial North America. Consequently, the English

language is a culmination of dialects, all originating from Arabic. This linguistic influence is also noticeable in French, Spanish, and Italian mathematical expressions. Similarly, both German and Jewish mathematical expressions bear striking similarities. This concrete evidence comprehensively clarifies the meaning behind the phrase "E pluribus unum" on U.S. colorable money: "Out of many, one."

As mentioned earlier, the English language has roots in various Latin dialects, all of which have Moorish origins. When people claim that English isn't their language, it underscores how the education system was designed to mislead and condition our collective minds. This has been a significant factor contributing to the issues faced by our people. Moorish individuals have been unknowingly distancing themselves from their own language.

English serves as a versatile tool for conveying messages from numerous perspectives. The term "angle" can also refer to a "viewpoint" and is related to the word "perspective." Much like many other human languages, English often provides multiple words to describe and define a concept, enabling us to comprehend it from various viewpoints, perspectives, or angles.

The English alphabet, which forms the basis of the language, originates from the Latin alphabet. What many aren't aware of is that the Latin alphabet was constructed using principles of sacred geometry, involving sacred numbers, lines, arcs, and angles. "Geometry" refers to the branch of mathematics dealing with the properties, measurements, and relationships of points, lines, angles, and figures in space, derived from specified properties of space.

A crucial term to decode in this context is "alphabet." It combines the Greek letters A/a, meaning "the first" or "beginning," and B/b (beta), signifying "the second letter of the Greek alphabet (B)." Interestingly, in astronomy, "alpha" is used to denote the brightest star in a constellation, while "beta" refers to the second brightest star.

The Greek letters alpha and beta trace their roots back to the Hebrew letters בא or alpeph-beth, where the first character means "ox" or "bull," and the latter signifies "house." According to the book "The Mysteries of the Alphabet," the Hebrew letter aleph conveys "strength" or "man," while beth symbolizes "house" and serves as a metaphor for the womb.[11] Aleph is closely associated with terms like father, man, and male, while Beth is linked to mother, woman, and female. It's important to note that the English letters A/a and B/b are also derived from the Hebrew letters aleph and beth, respectively. This is why the English letter "B," stemming from the Hebrew "beth" (meaning "house" and "womb"), resembles two breasts, "b."

On a deeper spiritual level, the alphabet's letters hold profound information about a polaric and divine narrative. This sacred tale revolves around the journey of achieving balance and harmony between the divine masculine and feminine energies, concealed within words, letters, and symbols. Within this narrative lie the universe's secrets and the authentic history of mankind. This divine story is intricately linked to the concept of Alpha and Omega, signifying the beginning

---

11. Marc-Alain Ouaknin, *Mysteries of the Alphabet: The Origins of Writing*, 1999.

and the end. In the Greek alphabet, Alpha is represented by the letter A, denoting the initial or first letter, while Omega is depicted by the letter Ω, signifying the final or last letter. It's worth noting that the New Testament of the Bible was originally penned using the Greek alphabet.

Throughout history, angels have often been portrayed as beings of light. An essential aspect of light is its electromagnetic waves, which embody the characteristics of both the divine masculine and feminine energies. This is evident when the term "electromagnetic" is deconstructed into two words, yielding the prefix "electro-" and the word "magnetic." Etymologically, "electro-" means "related to electricity," while "magnetic" signifies possessing the properties of a magnet. Electricity represents power and the Divine Masculine Energy, while magnetism embodies the Divine Feminine Energy. While these two forces may seem opposite, they are interdependent, as one cannot exist without the other.

The purpose of the alphabet is to convey the limitless expression of both divine masculine and feminine energies, enabling the materialization of polaric concepts like positive and negative, male and female, order and chaos, good and evil, etc. This explains why letters are organized into the term alphabet, where "alpha" embodies the masculine principle and "beta" embodies the feminine principle. This system of sacred symbols is employed by humanity to bring worlds into existence through the influential use of positive and negative words. Within the alphabet lies the concealed wisdom of the archangels.[12]

In Genesis 1:3, the Bible states, "and God said, let there be light: and there was light." This verse explicitly conveys that God employs words, logos, and sound to bring forth light. It's important to note that the term "light" is strongly intertwined with words like word,

---

12. Pao Chang, *Word Magic*, 6-8.

grammar, logos, and universe. In classical Greek philosophy, "logos" is defined as reason, seen as the governing principle of the universe and expressed through speech. This embodies sacred geometry. The proof of the logos word's influential power in creating mystical phenomena, including sacred geometry, is evident in the field of cymatics. The King James Bible says in Hebrews chapter 4:12 states:

> For the word of God is living and powerful, and sharper than any two edged sword, piercing even to the division of soul and spirit, and joints and marrow, and is a discerner of the thoughts and intents of the heart.

Numerous words have been introduced by dark forces as hypnotic symbols, with the aim of manipulating and controlling our minds. One source of these malevolent behaviors from dark forces is what's referred to as a "cosmic virus." This isn't your typical virus; it possesses a high level of intelligence. The primary objective of this cosmic virus is to spread its selfish and destructive thoughts to infect all living beings across the universe. Many individuals, particularly those exhibiting strong psychopathic traits, have succumbed to the selfish and destructive thoughts propagated by this cosmic virus.

Much like any virus, the cosmic virus aims to deplete its host's energy until it perishes, ultimately seeking to cause death and devastation throughout the universe. The encouraging news is that this virus can only infiltrate us when we exist in a state of ignorance, fear, hatred, and irresponsibility. As we work towards peaceful coexistence, nurture our bodies, and activate the higher elements of our DNA, our frequency will elevate beyond the reach of the cosmic virus, rendering us immune to its influence.[13]

---

13. Ibid

## Dark Spells

The elite have altered the first law of darkness with amendments, permitting the so-called Negro to learn how to read and write in this generation, as long as he consumes information that we provide for him, ensuring his indoctrination. This allows them to maintain control without the need for physical chains of bondage. The crucial shift lies in altering his mindset, inundating him with European history while neglecting to educate him about his own heritage. By portraying the champions of so-called Negro history as European, he will be led to believe he has never achieved anything of significance. They seek to establish the narrative that so-called Negro history only began in 1619 with the arrival of the kidnappers.

> *My people are destroyed for lack of knowledge: because thou hast rejected knowledge, I will also reject thee, that thou shall be no priest to me: seeing thou hast forgotten the law of thy God, I will also forget thy children.* Hosea 4:6

The powers that be fear your acquisition of knowledge, as with increased knowledge, the veil of darkness lifts from your eyes, enabling you to see more clearly. Consider, why was a workforce of 42 million so-called Negroes exploited for 392 years? If this method works, why not apply it globally? This is how the elite maintain control over the masses. Knowledge is indeed power. The mindset was to keep the so-called Negro in the dark, ensuring perpetual servitude. This was the prevailing mentality among Southern European slave owners. Today, the so-called Negro community in America finds itself in a similar condition. Educated in Western educational institutions, but educated in what? The grammar schools, high schools, and colleges in the United States have been designed for one purpose: to impart generations with falsehoods and indoctrinate them with a skewed history of European nations and people. They are taught to harbor self-hatred and resentment towards their own identity and those who resemble them.[14] Television, radio, sports, newspapers, concerts, parties, substance use, drug trade, gang activity—all of these factors contribute to keeping 42 million so-called Negroes in America from awakening. There was a time, even during so-called slavery, when the so-called Negro would brave great risks to learn how to read. Yet now, he has been relegated to a state of mental captivity.[15]

Lack of understanding regarding the scientific truths underlying the inner workings, actions, and reactions of beings, as depicted in the 12 signs of the Zodiac, leads to a state of confusion. This state of mind can result in mental, economic, and social hardships, often described as a form of "hell".

> Hell = The name formally given to a place under the exchequer chamber; Where the kings debtors were confined. [16]

A common misconception is that we're taught to believe hell is a distant place awaiting those who err. In truth, this earth can be both hell and heaven, but both states are primarily a matter of one's mindset. The genuine hell hasn't materialized yet, but it will. Similarly, with heaven or haven, neither was created by the Most High, but rather by man. Through our actions, we've turned paradise into a nightmare, teeming with all manner of debauchery that will ultimately lead to self-destruction. Hellish experiences are part of our daily lives, just as heavenly ones are. The pivotal question is which state we choose to dwell in. It all boils down to choices, and that is the gift of free will bestowed upon humanity.[17]

---

14. Lee Cummings, *The Negro Question Part 3 The Black Pentecost* (Createspace Independent Publishing Platform, 2014), 53.

15. Ibid,

16. Henry C. Black, "Hell," in *Black's Law Dictionary* (St. Paul, MN: West Publishing, 1951).

17. Mishaal Talib Mahfuz El Bey, *The Torch: A Guide to S.E.L.F.*, 204.

> *He who knows the enemy and himself will never in a hundred battles be at risk.* ~ Sun-Tzu, Fourth Century B.C

Innerstand that words hold immense power and can be wielded for both positive and negative purposes. It's crucial to maintain constant awareness in order to shield yourself from both visible and hidden forces.

The term "black," when applied to Moors, is not just a label, but a weaponized term. Its purpose is not only to denationalize, but even worse, to dehumanize. Labels like "colored," "African American," "Indian," and "person of color" are social constructs imposed on Moorish people, engineered by European colonists and supported by their Caucasian counterparts. This status places individuals at the lowest rung of the political hierarchy, symbolizing the marginalized of society. Unfortunately, many of the original inhabitants of this hemisphere have internalized this spirit, leading to feelings of anger, jealousy, greed, and hatred. They find themselves essentially dead in both civil and mental aspects, blinded by ignorance and disconnected from the truth.

Even our brothers and sisters from other nations contribute to perpetuating this deception. They come here, setting up businesses, taking advantage of our ignorance, much like the Romans of old, feeding on our vulnerabilities like vultures. Interestingly, on their passports, they hold the status of "white." Of course, they never reveal this to us, as they fear we might reject them. Some even strike secret deals with the Jesuits to keep our true identity hidden, all the while laughing at us behind our backs.

To put it plainly, if you accept or claim the label "black," without correction, you are, in the eyes of the universe—both seen and unseen—agreeing to servitude and spiritual death.[18]

---

18. Ibid, 200.

Linguistically, we can easily deduce that the term "black" has its roots in Middle English "blak," Old English "blaec," Old High German "blah," Latin "flagrare," and Greek "phlegein." Over time, it has undergone various transformations, evolving into its modern form. Given that "black" emerged in modern English, it suggests that it wasn't used to refer to people before the 1100s to 1400s or during the pre-Columbian era. To put it simply, the term didn't exist and therefore couldn't have had a definitive application to people, nor a place in the context of any spoken or written languages prior to the pre-Columbian civilization.

## Modern English excludes African and Aboriginal Languages.

The most ancient names for so-called black people include Nehesu or Nubian, Ethiopian, and Moor, originating from ancient Egypt. Additionally, terms like Negro or Nigrita come from West Africa, all of which are native African words. On the contrary, "black" and "white" as terms for color originate from Europe. Ethiopian and Moor were commonly used to describe so-called blacks until around 1500. Shakespeare, for instance, employs the term "Negro" only once, using it synonymously with Moor.[19]

Gradually, another association took hold in North America, linking the term "negro" with "slave". Early legislation often referred to "negro and other slaves", or to "negro, mulatto, and Indian slaves". As time passed, both "negro" and "black" became synonymous with enslavement.

In 1802, an observer noted that the wealth of Virginia largely consisted of slaves or negros. In 1806, Virginia judges decreed that

---

19. J. A. Rogers, *100 Amazing Facts About the Negro with Complete Proof: A Short Cut to The World History of The Negro* (Wesleyan University Press, 1995), 91.

a person with a so-called white appearance was to be presumed free, but in the case of a person visibly appearing to be of the slave race, the burden of proof fell on him to establish his freedom. In 1819, South Carolina judges unequivocally stated: "The word 'negroes' has a fixed meaning (slaves)."[20]

It should be kept in mind that in the 1600s, the term "negro" could refer to both Asians and Africans (or individuals of African descent). At times, a performer in pageants would be identified as one or the other, or their costume would offer a clue. However, so-called black performers were often asked to portray "American Indians."[21]

---

20. Jack D. Forbes, *Africans and Native Americans: The Language of Race and the Evolution of Red-Black Peoples* (University of Illinois Press, 1993), 84.

21. Ibid, 85.

# End Notes

Bey, Uriel, and Princeps Uriel-Bai. *The Consecrated Talisman: "Salmagundi,"* 2010.

Black, Henry C. "Hell." In *Black's Law Dictionary*. St. Paul, MN: West Publishing, 1951.

Chang, Pao. *Word Magic: The Powers and Occult Definitions of Words* (Second Edition). Esoteric Knowledge Publishing, 2019.

Cummings, Lee. *The Negro Question Part 3 The Black Pentecost*. Createspace Independent Publishing Platform, 2014.

Forbes, Jack D. *Africans and Native Americans: The Language of Race and the Evolution of Red-Black Peoples*. University of Illinois Press, 1993.

Bible Gateway. "King James Version." Accessed June 3, 2023. https://www.biblegateway.com/passage/?search=Numbers+32%3A37-38&version=KJV.

Mahfuz El Bey, Mishaal Talib. *The Torch: A Guide to S.E.L.F*. Califa Media Publishing, 2020.

"Mowreh Hebrew Meaning - Old Testament Lexicon (KJV)." In *Biblestudytools*.Com. Accessed July 10, 2023. https://www.biblestudytools.com/lexicons/hebrew/kjv/mowreh-2.html.

Najee-Ullah El, Tauheedah S., ed. "Koran Questions for Moorish Americans: 101s And Additional Laws." In *Califa Uhuru: A Compilation of Literature from the Moorish Science Temple of America*. Califa Media Publishing, 2014.

Ouaknin, Marc-Alain. Mysteries of the Alphabet: The Origins of Writing, 1999.

Rogers, J. A. 100 Amazing Facts About the Negro with Complete Proof: A Short Cut to The World History of The Negro. Wesleyan University Press, 1995.

Wikiwand. "Wikiwand - Mesha Stele," n.d. https://www.wikiwand.com/en/Mesha_Stele.

# Notes

# Chapter 4

## The Dangers of Color

### COLOR

An appearance, semblance, or simulacrum, as distinguished from that which is real. A prima facie or apparent right. Hence, a deceptive appearance; a plausible, assumed exterior, concealing a lack of reality; a disguise or pretext Railroad Co. v. Allfree, 64 Iowa, 500, 20 N. W. 779; Berks County v. Railroad Co., 167 Pa. 102, 31 Atl. 474; Broughton v. Haywood, 61 N. C 383.

In pleading: Ground of action admitted to subsist in the opposite party by the pleading of one of the parties to an action, which is so set out as to be apparently valid, but which is in reality legally insufficient. This was a term of the ancient rhetoricians, and early adopted into the language of pleading. It was an apparent or prima facie right; and the meaning of the rule that pleadings in confession and avoidance should give color was that they should confess the matter adversely alleged, to such an extent, at least as to admit some apparent right in the opposite party, which required to be encountered and avoided by the allegation of new matter. Color was either express, i.e. if inserted in the pleading, or implied, which was naturally inherent in the structure of the pleading. Steph. Pl. 233; Merten v. Bank, 5 Okl. 585, 49 Pac. 933. The word also means the dark color of the skin showing the presence of negro blood; and hence it is equivalent to African descent or parentage.[1]

### COLORABLE

Ostensibly appearing as something which, it is not, a deceptive appearance. Alternative Legal Definition: That which has or gives color. That which is in appearance only, and not in reality, what it purports to be. Colorable alteration. One which makes no real or substantial change, but is introduced only as a subterfuge or means of

---

1. "Color | Black's Law 2d Ed," in *Internet Archive*, 2010, accessed July 5, 2023, https://archive.org/details/BlacksLaw2dEd.

*evading the patent or copyright law. Colorable imitation. In the law of trademarks, this phrase denotes such a close or ingenious imitation as to be calculated to deceive ordinary persons. Colorable pleading. The practice of giving color in pleading.*²

## COLORED Definition & Legal Meaning

*By common usage in America, this term, in such phrases as "colored persons," "the colored race," "colored men," and the like, is used to designate negroes or persons of the African race, including all persons of mixed blood descended from negro ancestry.* <u>Van Camp v. Board of Education</u>, *9 Ohio St. 411;* <u>U. S. v. La Coste</u>, *20 Fed. Cas. S29;* <u>Jones v. Com.</u>, *80 Va. 542;* <u>Heirn v. Bridault</u>, *37 Miss. 222;* <u>State v. Chavers</u>, *50 N. C. 15;* <u>Johnson v. Norwich</u>, *29 Conn. 407.*³

The truth is that individuals who identify as "colored persons" face challenges because no judicial court is obligated to respect them. Their persistent association with terms that carry historical connotations of slavery is the reason they have never received, and likely will never receive, justice.

## Christian Black Codes – Codes Noir (1724)

As previously mentioned, the word "black" translates to "noir" in French. Consequently, through the stroke of a pen, Europeans composed documents that inflicted political and civic terror upon the Moorish people. This ultimately culminated in the formulation of the Christian Black Codes, or Codes Noir, in 1724. Below are paraphrased versions and observations of some of its articles:

**Article 1:** Declares the expulsion of the Jews from the colony—keep in mind that the word "Jew" is a misnomer for the Moors.

---

2. Ibid, "Colorable."

3. Henry C. Black, "Colored," in *Black's Law Dictionary* (St. Paul, MN: West Publishing, 1951).

**Article 2:** Makes it incumbent upon masters to impart "religious" instruction to their slaves.

*side note* This is why the churches demand their followers have blind faith and frown upon those who ask questions.

**Article 3:** Permits the exercise of the Roman Catholic creed only — every other mode of worship is prohibited.

* side note* This goes right along with the Manifest Destiny, Magna Carter, Church Bullas, and the Doctrine of Discovery exposing how European Christianity was forced on the so-called black slaves, and did not originate with their forefathers in the form practiced today.

**Article 4:** Negroes placed under the direction of supervision of any person other than a Catholic, are liable to confiscation.

*side note* This goes to the programming of no-one-can-tell-me-anything-but-a-European.

**Article 5:** Sundays and holidays are to be strictly observed. All negroes found at work on these days are to be confiscated.

*side note* This should clarify the origin of the idea that slaves, with unwavering faith and dedication, gathered in their masters' churches on Sundays. It also sheds light on why these slaves subsequently self-righteously accused the prophets of the East of condoning such practices.

**Article 52:** We declare that the acts for the enfranchisement of slaves, passed according to the forms above described, shall be equivalent on an act of naturalization, when said slaves are not born in our colony of Louisiana, and they shall enjoy all the rights and privileges inherent to our subjects born in our kingdoms, or in any land or colony under dominion. We declare, however, that all manumitted slaves, and all freeborn ******* are incapable of receiving donations, either by testimony dispositions or by acts inter vivos from the whites.

Ch.4

Said donation shall be null and void, and the objects of said donation shall be applied to the benefits of the nearest hospital.

*side note* Article 15 of the Christian Black Codes forms the basis for the de facto, ex post facto, unconstitutional, and fraudulent assertion that slaves are citizens of the U.S.A., constituting a civil rights fraud regarding the 14th and 15th amendments. Those well-versed in the law are knowledgeable about these facts.

The church employs its ordinances or Canon laws to govern the oppressed Moors, while the states utilize de facto ordinances or Canon laws to exploit and govern the oppressed Moors labeled as black, colored, negro, Puerto Rican, Latino, Hispanic, Indian, etc. There has never been a separation between church and state; they are inherently intertwined.

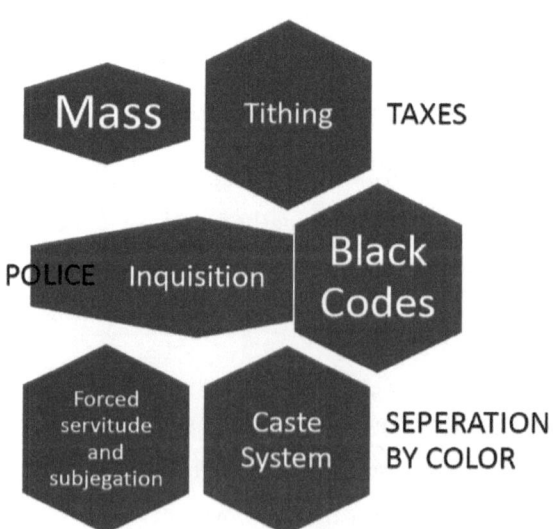

# THE INVISIBLE PRISON

Much like in a Broadway play, musical, or movie, where cast members become closely associated with their characters and may even be typecast, confined to either inflated or disfavored assumptions, they can eventually embody their characters. As an actor, you are expected to move and speak as directed by your role. You are not portraying yourself; you are becoming your character. Adhere strictly to the script and your designated role, and you will receive rewards. Deviate from it, and you'll face consequences. If you stray from the script, fellow cast members may step in to guide you back. Should this occur frequently or at a crucial juncture, you might be terminated, demoted, excluded, or conveniently written out of the plot with your character meeting its end.[4]

The social hierarchy, often referred to as a caste system, is not equivalent to the cast and the play, although the resemblance between the two terms is intriguing. When we're assigned roles, we cease to be ourselves. It's not expected of us to be our true selves. Instead, we perform based on our position in the production, not necessarily reflecting our inner selves. We all function as actors on a stage that was constructed long before our ancestors set foot on this land. We are the most recent cast in a longstanding drama that first debuted on this soil in the early 17th century.[5]

In the corporate United States, there exists an unspoken race-based caste system pyramid. This system stigmatizes those considered inferior, providing a justification for the dehumanization required to maintain the lowest-ranking individuals at the bottom and to legitimize enforcement protocols. The caste hierarchy is not based on feelings or

---

4. Isabel Wilkerson, Caste: The Origins of Our Discontents (Random House, 2020), 40.
5. Ibid.

morality, but on power — which groups possess it, and which do not.6 In the American caste system, the marker of rank is what we refer to as race, which involves categorizing humans based on their appearance. In America, race serves as the primary tool and the conspicuous distraction, effectively acting as the spokesperson for caste.7

Race serves as the primary mechanism for a caste system that requires a means of human division. If we've been conditioned to perceive humans through the lens of race, then caste is the underlying framework ingrained in us from childhood, much like learning our mother tongue. Similar to grammar, caste becomes an imperceptible guide not only in how we communicate, but also in how we process information, making automatic calculations that contribute to a sentence without conscious thought.

We may make reference to race, using terms like black, white, Latino, Asian, or indigenous. However, beneath each label lies centuries of history, laden with assumptions and values attributed to physical attributes within a structure of human hierarchy. What people look like, or more accurately, the race they have been assigned or are perceived to belong to, provides a visible clue to their caste.[8]

In the same manner that terms like "black" and "white" were applied to individuals who were not literally so, but rather shades of brown, beige, and ivory, the caste system places people at poles from one another and assigns significance to the extremes and the gradations in between. It then reinforces these meanings, replicating them in the roles each caste was and is assigned, as well as permitted or required to perform.

Caste and race are neither synonymous nor mutually exclusive. They can and do coexist in the same culture, serving to reinforce each other.

---

6. Ibid, 17.
7. Ibid, 18.
8. Ibid.

In the United States, race acts as the visible agent of the unseen force of caste. Caste forms the structural framework, while race constitutes the visible characteristics. Race encompasses the physical traits to which arbitrary meanings have been assigned, becoming shorthand for a person's identity. Caste is the potent infrastructure that maintains each group in its designated position.

Caste remains fixed and rigid, whereas race is fluid and superficial, subject to periodic redefinition to suit the needs of the dominant caste in what is now referred to as the de facto United States. While the criteria to be considered "white" have evolved over the centuries, the existence of a dominant caste has been constant since its inception. However, whoever fit the definition of "so-called white" at any given point in history was granted the legal rights and privileges of the dominant caste. Tragically, at the opposite end of the spectrum, the subordinate caste has been set from the outset as the psychological floor beneath which all other castes cannot fall.[9]

Much like the hidden framework of a building comprised of studs, joints, and beams, caste operates in a similar fashion. Its very invisibility empowers it and ensures its endurance. Though it may ebb and flow in public consciousness, surfacing prominently during times of upheaval and receding in periods of relative calm, it remains a steady foundation in the functioning of the country. The term "caste" is not commonly employed in discussions about the United States. It is more frequently associated with India or feudal Europe. U.S. Senator Charles Sumner is quoted as saying, "Caste makes distinctions where God has made none."

The social economist Gunnar Myrdal and his team of accomplished researchers produced a two-volume work spanning 2,800 pages, still widely regarded as perhaps the most comprehensive study of race in America, titled "An American Dilemma." They determined that the

9. Ibid, 19.

most accurate term to describe the workings of American society was not "race," but "caste." It was, in their view, possibly the only term that adequately addressed the seemingly entrenched hierarchy of human value. Myrdal concluded that America had established a caste system, and that the task of maintaining the color line, to the average so-called white man, was the very function of upholding that caste system itself — of ensuring that the "Negro" stayed in his designated place. In 1942, he wrote, "When we speak of the race problem in America, what we really mean is the caste system and the problems which the caste system creates in America."[10]

> "Race is a social concept, not a scientific one." Geneticist J. Craig Venter

Caste is structure. Caste is ranking. Caste is the boundaries that reinforce fixed assignments based on appearance. It's a living, breathing entity, akin to a corporation that strives to sustain itself at any cost.

Caste involves the granting or withholding of respect, status, honor, attention, privileges, resources, benefit of the doubt, and human kindness to someone based on their perceived rank or standing in the hierarchy.

Caste is insidious and powerful because it's not rooted in hatred, nor is it necessarily personal. It's the well-worn grooves of familiar routines and thoughtless expectations, patterns of a social order that have been in place for so long that they appear as the natural order of things.

Distinguishing between racism and casteism can be challenging due to the intertwined nature of caste and race in America. Any action or institution that ridicules, harms, assumes, or attaches inferiority or stereotypes based on the social construct of race can be considered racism. On the other hand, any action or structure that seeks to

---

10. Ibid, 22-23.

restrict, hold back, or categorize someone, aiming to keep them in a defined position by elevating or generating that person based on their perceived category, can be viewed as casteism.

Oppressed people from various parts of the world, especially from Europe, passed through Ellis Island, shedding their old identities, and often their old names, to gain entry into the powerful dominant majority. Somewhere in this journey, these Europeans underwent a transformation they had never experienced or needed before. They transitioned from being Czech, Hungarian, or Polish to being labeled as "white" – a political designation that only holds meaning when contrasted with something not "white". They joined a new entity, an encompassing category for anyone arriving in the New World from Europe. According to immigration and legal scholar Ian Haney Lopez, Germans were accepted as part of the dominant caste in the 1840s, followed by the Irish in the 1850s to 1880s, and the Eastern and Southern Europeans in the early twentieth century. It was in becoming American that they became white.[11]

"In Ireland or Italy," Lopez noted, "whatever social or racial identities these people might have possessed, being 'white' wasn't one of them." Serbs and Albanians, Swedes and Russians, Turks and Bulgarians – who may have been at odds with each other in their home countries – were fused together not on the basis of shared ethnic culture, language, faith, or national origin, but solely on the basis of their appearance, all to bolster the dominant caste in the hierarchy.[12]

*"No one was white before he/she came to America,"* James Baldwin

In order to gain acceptance, each new wave of immigrants had to enter into an unspoken agreement to separate and distance themselves from the established lowest caste. Becoming "white" meant defining

---

11. "Isabel Wilkerson on the Legacies of American Chattel Slavery," Literary Hub, December 4, 2020, https://lithub.com/isabel-wilkerson-on-the-legacies-of-american-chattel-slavery/.
12. Ibid.

themselves as being furthest from its opposite — "black." They could solidify their new status by observing how the lowest caste was treated, and by imitating or surpassing the disdain and contempt, learning the derogatory terms, and even participating in acts of violence against them to prove their worthiness for admission into the dominant caste.

> "Africans are not black," she explained. "They are Igbo and Yoruba, Ewe, Akan, Ndebele. They are not black. They are just themselves. They are humans on the land. This is how they see themselves, and that is who they are." What we consider to be fundamental truths in American culture are foreign to them, she pointed out. "They don't become black until they go to America or come to the UK," she said. "It is then that they become black."[13]

It was through the establishment of a new world that Europeans became "white," Africans became "black," and everyone else was categorized as "yellow," "red," or "brown." It was in the formation of the so-called New World that humans were set apart based on their appearance, defined solely in contrast to one another, and ranked to establish a caste system rooted in a new concept known as race. It was in the process of ranking that we were all assigned roles to fulfill the needs of the larger production, none of us determining our roles ourselves.

The Statue of Liberty on Bedloe's Island in New York Bay was designed by Bartholdi and was a gift from the free citizens of the Union states. It was dedicated to the victorious Daughters of the American Revolution who defeated the Moral Society of Islam. The statue was completed in 1886. On Ellis Island, all "white" foreigners are instructed to uphold the myth of so-called white supremacy in the Union states before they are eligible for citizenship in the good old U.S.A. [14]

---

13. Ibid.
14. Charles Mosely Bey, *Clock of Destiny 1 & 2*, Paperback (Moorish National Order of the Great Seal of 360 Degrees, 1947), 23.

*Marigot, St. Martin*
*Source: Adventures in Gigi*

*Blackamoor Figure, Artist Unknown*
*Source Unknown*

Now look at the crown of the above picture. This Moorish influence is/was undoubtedly in the Americas as well as every square inch of the entire world.

Let's take a look at the at the original Statue of Liberty...

The Statue of Liberty Was Originally a Moorish woman. The sketch of Bartholdi's proposal for the Suez Canal shows a Muslim woman wearing traditional Arab clothing. That might be surprising to people more familiar with the statue's French roots than its Arab ones.

*The Statue of Liberty Is Egyptian.*
*FoulForaFool.com*

### Race

*An ethnical stock; A great division of mankind having in common certain distinguishing physical peculiarities constituting a comprehensive class appear to be derived from a distinct primitive source a tribal or national stock, a division or subdivision of one of the great racial stocks of mankind distinguished by minor peculiarities. Descent. <u>In re Halladjian</u>, C.C. Mass., 174 F. 834; <u>Ex parte (Ng.) Fung Sing</u>, D.C. Wash., I 6 F. 2nd 670< Old French rais or raiz < Latin radix, root.* [15]

There is only one race on this planet, and that is the human race. As mentioned prior in this manuscript, all beings on this planet trace their origins back to the great Moabite woman, the matriarch and progenitor of the human family. This is an indisputable fact, even acknowledged by modern archaeologists who readily affirm that all life on this planet stems from what they refer to as the African woman—some scholars have even called them zodiacs.

The term "primitive," according to the 1973 World Book Dictionary, means of early times; belonging to a distant past; first of its kind; very simple; original; primary; and primordial. It comes from the Latin word "primitivus," which is derived from "primitiae," meaning first things or first fruits, and ultimately from "Primus," meaning first. In society, the term "primitive" is often associated with Neanderthals or cave dwellers, which can be seen as a form of disrespect towards the wisdom and achievements of ancient civilizations. It attempts to marginalize the contributions of these ancient civilizations and assert an unwarranted importance of hybrids, who don't truly have a significant place in the narrative. We, as Asiatics, are the original and natural people of this planet. We gave birth, both naturally and through various forms of artificial means, to all other peoples on this planet. It's important to note that the term "Negro" used for slaves differs from the term "Negroes" used as a color designation.

---

15. Black, "Race," in *Black's Law Dictionary*.

### Excerpt from "The Illusion of Races":

*With the word "race" it happened as with the word "Negro" which was extended through Europe and America from Portugal and Spain by the traders in African slaves since the 15th century. Before that time there had been used in several European languages, including those of Iberia the respective words indicative of dark color of pigmentation in order to designate black slaves, blacks in English and noirs in French. When the trade spread, there prevailed in these lands other words derive from Hispano-Portuguese negro, such as nigger in English and negre in French, And all these words had a contemptuous meaning as related to slavery. Even today in the French language a distinction is made between the words noir and negre; as in English black is differentiated from nigger and from negro.[16]*

The so-called "black race" does not actually exist; this categorization was theorized by Johann Frederick Blumenbach, a German scientist. In 1779, he divided the human species into five races based on cranial research and descriptions of human skulls:

- The Caucasian or white race;
- The Mongolian or yellow race, including all east Asians and some central Asians;
- The Malayan or brown race, including Southeast Asian and Pacific Islanders;
- The Ethiopian or black race, including sub-Saharan Africans;
- The American or red race including American Indians.

Propaganda and confusion are some of the weapons of mass deception used by the hybrid Europeans and those working with the Dark forces. The U.S. Census Bureau must adhere to the 1997 Office

---

16. "RACE - The Power of an Illusion . Ask the Experts | PBS," n.d., https://www.pbs.org/race/000_About/002_04-experts-03-03.htm.

of Management and Budget (OMB) standards on race and ethnicity which guide the Census Bureau in classifying written responses to the race question:

White: A person having origins in any of the original peoples of Europe, the Middle East, or North Africa.

Black or African American: A person having origins in any of the Black racial groups of Africa.

In order to comprehend this paper genocide we have to go first to the origin of it's creation.

## When was the census created?

The United States census also played a role in the use and definition of terms like "black" and "negro." In 1890, "black" was to be used for individuals with 3/4 or more black blood. In 1910, "blacks" were meant for full-blooded 'negroes,' while the determination of who was considered Indian was left to the enumerator. In the 1910 census, there were "2,255 negroes" who had some Indian heritage and were enrolled members of tribes. By 1930, a person with mixed Indian and Negro heritage was to be classified as a "negro" unless the Indian blood was more prominent and their status as an Indian was widely accepted in the community. By 1940, all African American hybrids were to be counted as "negroes" unless their Indian ancestry overwhelmingly prevailed and they were universally recognized as Indians. Thus, by 1940, ALL so-called Indians, mulattos, etc. were classified as so-called "negroes."

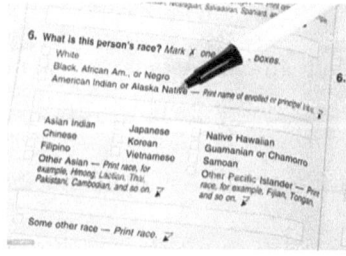

*Census Form*
*Blackwater Images/ Getty Images*

Even pure-blooded Indians could be counted as blacks, as was the case in Nevada in 1880 when 90 members of the Duck Water

Shoshone Tribe were categorized in that way. In Delaware in more recent decades, if a person claimed to be Indian, they were recorded as either black or white depending on their appearance. Instructions for the 1980 census stated that any person who checked both the black and Indian boxes would be counted solely as black. However, during oral interviews, the race mentioned first for the respondent's mother would hold more significance. A long list of countries was provided to census takers, with specific categories for counting rather than using the country name. A significant number of countries, including Trinidad and nearly all of the West Indies, were arbitrarily assigned to the black category. Consequently, Americans with roots in places like Aruba, Trinidad, or Dominica would be counted as blacks.

Notably, not a single country, including Guatemala, Bolivia, Peru, and Paraguay, was categorized under the Indian category. It's evident that the census methods in 1980 had the impact of downplaying the count of Indians. This can be corroborated by referring to the Race and Ethnic Standards for Federal Statistics and Administrative Reporting.[17]

The U.S. CORPORATION uses the census forms to categorize and group the aboriginal indigenous people from North, Central, South America and all the adjoining islands into BLACK which denationalizes them collectively. Unbeknownst to them this is genocide.

## What is genocide?

The 1948 convention on the prevention and punishment of the crime of genocide known as the "Genocide Convention" defines genocide as any of the following acts committed with the intent to destroy, in whole or in part, a national, ethnical, racial or religious group:[18]

---

17. "OMB DIRECTIVE 15: RACE AND ETHNIC STANDARDS FOR FEDERAL STATISTICS AND ADMINISTRATIVE REPORTING," n.d., https://wonder.cdc.gov/wonder/help/populations/bridged-race/directive15.html.

18. United Nations General Assembly, ed., *Convention on the Prevention and Punishment of the Crime of Genocide* (United Nations Office on Genocide Prevention & Responsibility to Protect, 1948).

- Killing members of the group;
- Causing serious bodily or mental harm to members of the group;
- Deliberately inflicting on the group the conditions of life calculated to bring about its physical destruction in whole or part;
- Imposing measures intended to prevent births within the group;
- Forcibly transferring children of the group to another group.

Here are examples of genocide:

- Police terrorism mislabeled police brutality
- Planned Parenthood;
- Family court;
- Child Protective Services;
- Department of Child, Youth, and Family;
- GMOS;
- Fluoride in the water supply;
- Gentrification;
- Slave movies and the like showing aboriginal indigenous peoples being tortured, beat, terrorized etc. (mental warfare);
- Televised denationalization programming (propaganda);

## What is terrorism?

*...the unlawful use of violence or threats to intimidate or coerce a civilian population or government, with the goal of furthering political, social, or ideological objectives.*[19]

*The state of fear and submission produced by terrorism.*[20]

---

19. Gregor Bruce, "Definition of Terrorism," JMVH, May 26, 2023, accessed June 6, 2023.
20. "Terrorism Definition & Meaning," in *Dictionary.Com*, September 11, 2020, accessed June 6, 2023.

The ongoing debate about race serves as a diversion not intended to tackle the actual problem at hand. The true issue is genocide. Everything else amounts to socially engineered smoke and mirrors, a form of misdirection crafted to maintain the faith of the masses, keeping them moving forward in a state of prayer, hope, and pleas for change. Real change will occur when we shift our mindsets and collectively assume responsibility for our actions and affairs.

## Light (Knowledge) and Darkness (Ignorance)

The United States Corporation is guilty of crafting the narrative of human trafficking, dividing people into so-called white and black, all for the purpose of control and enslavement.

The Bible states, "And God said, 'Let there be light,' and there was light. God saw that the light was good, and he separated the light from the darkness. God called the light 'day,' and the darkness he called 'night.' And there was evening, and there was morning—the first day." (Genesis chapter 1: 3-5). These concepts were also present before the existence of the Garden of Eden. What is this light? Could it be the same light that all Freemasons spend their lives searching for? Yeshua said, "Light is but the breath of Allah vibrating in the rhythm of rapid thought." (Appendix; Life of Joshua, 18; 11). The darkness, on the other hand, is the absence of this light, vibrating at a much slower pace. From the very start, light and darkness existed, before spiritual man had a concept of time. In all holy books, those meant to guide humanity, reference is made to light or darkness, which undoubtedly applies to levels of enlightenment, wisdom, or unconsciousness, representing human knowledge and ignorance.

With this comprehension, it becomes clear that the foundation of today's "skin game" was established as a measure to determine how close or distant a man is from the truth. The more godlike a man's pursuits, the closer he would be to embodying the light. Conversely, the further he delved into human thoughts, the deeper into the darkness of his mind he would lose himself. It's important to note here that the divine origin of light and darkness had absolutely nothing to do with skin color.

Today, the terms light and darkness have been misinterpreted as white and black, and are utilized to segregate people based on their ethnicity. Ironically, this is how the pale-skinned nations of Europe manipulate their Bible to elevate the white man as a God and label the black man as the opposite. Europeans reconstructed history, claiming they descended from cavemen rather than acknowledging the Garden of Eden, and tragically, the world bought into this falsehood.[21]

> In the Quran's Surah 3:106, it speaks of the black face and white face. Yusef Ali's commentary #432 reads, the 'face' (wajh) expresses our personality, our inmost being. White is the color of light to become white is to be illuminated with light, with Felicity in the rays of the glorious light wisdom of Allah. Black is the color of darkness sin rebellion and misery; Remove from the grace and the light of Allah there are signs of heaven and hell a standard of decision in all questions is the justice of Allah.[22]

Unfortunately, in this part of the continent identity is viewed or associated with the complexion whereby the hue of a man, due to social engineering, create certain type of perception and stigmatism. Both terms white and black are in actuality legal statuses in other words spells that invoke either the spirit of sovereignty or servitude. White means purity, purity means God and God is the ruler of the land. However being that Europeans are aliens they cannot truly be sovereign, or rulers of this land except by way of consent of the true heirs and sovereigns. Every time you call a European "white" or when

---

21. Elihu N. Pleasant-Bey, Noble Drew Ali, the Last Prophet: The Exhuming of a Nation (Seven Seals Publication, 2009), 350-351.
22. Ibid, 36.

Europeans accept and refer to themselves as white, both parties have committed an error in law and are co conspirators to fraud. Both have fallen in love with the lie.

Before the early and late 1800s, Europeans were not even referred to as "white." This designation was adopted through the Naturalization Act of 1790 on March 26, which was later amended in 1870. The term "black" was introduced during the Reconstruction Era after the systematic defeat of the Moors in a series of wars, both tribal and otherwise. The legal designation of the term "white" is actually rooted in astrology, referencing white light. White light is considered the highest because it encompasses all colors of the spectrum. Thus, the original concept of the Moorish term "white person" denoted a complete being, someone in good standing. The seven primordial planetary spheres of this galaxy combine to form white light. Seven is the number representing the perfect man. Therefore, to be "white" is to be a holistic being, one that embodies the divine essence and, in turn, reflects the boundless expanse of the universe.

Very few individuals on this planet truly merit this title. Most who use it are, for the most part, unqualified. This means that assuming it as a label without living up to the responsibilities of that vibration is an act of dishonor, as it is an insincere portrayal.

Light means knowledge — Knowledge is power — it spells Freedom — Freedom is everybody's responsibility on a universal scale.

According to Lobsang Rampa in "Wisdom of The Ancients," there are three prerequisites for attaining knowledge:[23]

Firstly, we must have inference. We need to become aware of something, as without awareness, we cannot perceive its presence or existence.

Secondly, we require reliable information. Without dependable

---

23. T. Lobsang Rampa, *Wisdom of the Ancients* (Important Books, 2013).

information to support our inferences, we have not even begun the journey towards acquiring knowledge.

Lastly, we need a form of institution to help us comprehend what lies beyond the matter we've inferred and for which we've obtained reliable information. This intuition is essential for understanding different aspects we wish to explore.

The mentality of a slave stems from a consistent diet of oppression and hypocrisy, with a dash of truth oddly mixed in. The free minds of the Moorish don't think like those who are mentally enslaved. So-called black people have been led to believe they're receiving education (erudition), but in reality, the longer they stay in the school systems, the longer the invisible veil remains over their God Eye. Mental chains are some of the most difficult to detect because people often aren't even aware they're there.

# End Notes

Black, Henry C. "Colored." In *Black's Law Dictionary*. St. Paul, MN: West Publishing, 1951.

———. "Race." In *Black's Law Dictionary*. St. Paul, MN: West Publishing, 1951.

Bruce, Gregor. "Definition of Terrorism." JMVH, May 26, 2023. Accessed June 6, 2023. https://jmvh.org/article/definitionof-terrorism-social-and-political-effects/.

"Color | Black's Law 2d Ed." In *Internet Archive*, 2010. Accessed July 5, 2023. https://archive.org/details/BlacksLaw2dEd.

Literary Hub. "Isabel Wilkerson on the Legacies of American Chattel Slavery," December 4, 2020. https://lithub.com/isabel-wilkerson-on-the-legacies-of-american-chattel-slavery/.

Mosely Bey, Charles. *Clock of Destiny 1 & 2*. Paperback. Moorish National Order of the Great Seal of 360 Degrees, 1947.

"OMB DIRECTIVE 15: RACE AND ETHNIC STANDARDS FOR FEDERAL STATISTICS AND ADMINISTRATIVE REPORTING," n.d. https://wonder.cdc.gov/wonder/help/populations/bridged-race/directive15.html.

Pleasant-Bey, Elihu N. *Noble Drew Ali, the Last Prophet: The Exhuming of a Nation*. Seven Seals Publication, 2009.

"RACE - The Power of an Illusion . Ask the Experts | PBS," n.d. https://www.pbs.org/race/000_About/002_04-experts-03-03.htm.

Rampa, T. Lobsang. *Wisdom of the Ancients*. Important Books, 2013.

"Terrorism Definition & Meaning." In Dictionary.Com, September 11, 2020. Accessed June 6, 2023. https://www.dictionary.com/browse/terrorism.

United Nations General Assembly, ed. *Convention on the Prevention and Punishment of the Crime of Genocide*. United Nations Office on Genocide Prevention & Responsibility to Protect, 1948. https://www.un.org/en/genocideprevention/genocide-convention.shtml.

Wilkerson, Isabel. *Caste: The Origins of Our Discontents*. Random House, 2020.

# Notes

# Chapter 5

## What is Belief?

> **Dictionary**
> Definitions from Oxford Languages · Learn more
>
>  be·lief
>
> *noun*
> 1. an acceptance that a statement is true or that something exists.
>    "his **belief in** the value of hard work"
> 2. trust, faith, or confidence in someone or something.
>    "I've still got belief in myself"

*Google Search: from Oxford Languages*

### What is faith?

NOUN

1. complete trust or confidence in someone or something:

"this restores one's faith in politicians"

2. strong belief in God or in the doctrines of a religion, based on spiritual apprehension rather than proof: o a system of religious belief:

or a strongly held belief or theory:

"bereaved people who have shown supreme faith"

"the Christian faith"

"the faith that life will expand until it fills the universe" [1]

The Holy Bible contains a clear definition of faith in Hebrews 11:1: "Now faith is the assurance of things hoped for, the conviction of things not seen." Simply put, the biblical definition of faith is "trusting in something you cannot explicitly prove."

---

1. "Faith Definition & Meaning" in *Dictionary.Com*, September 16, 2020, https://www.dictionary.com/browse/faiths.

**What is fruition?**

NOUN

1. the point at which a plan or project is realized: or the realization of a plan or project:

"the plans have come to fruition sooner than expected"

"new methods will come with the fruition of that research"[2]

No matter how strong someone's beliefs, convictions, or faith may be, without fruition (knowledge), they simply don't know. This is when they delve into their feelings, expressing opinions that do not necessarily equate to truth or facts. Noble Drew Ali consistently advised the Moors, stating, "If I can get you to think, you will save yourself." He further emphasized, "A slave will not proclaim himself, while a God-Man perceives freedom as a birthright and natural obligation."

It is crucial to remember that ignorance (darkness) is not determined by skin complexion but rather by a state of unconsciousness. Elevating one's consciousness is the key, the master grip, to salvation for those referred to as people of color, Latinos, Indians, and others who believe they are already free. The initial step towards correction involves addressing colorable slave laws, which begins with asserting a free national name and acknowledging one's birthright (identity).

*What is nationality?*

*What is identity?*

*What does proclaiming a national name mean?*

NATIONALITY: That quality or character which arises from the fact of a person's belonging to a nation or state. Nationality determines the political status of the individual, especially with reference to allegiance, while domicile determines his civil status.[3]

---

2. Ibid, "Fruition Definition & Meaning"

3. "Nationality," in *The Law Dictionary*, November 9, 2011, accessed June 6, 2023, https://thelawdictionary.org/identity..

As you can see, the word "status" is also referenced in the term "nationality." The significance of both status and nationality cannot be overstated. Therefore, it is important to consider why these topics are not discussed on major media outlets. The deliberate exclusion and suppression of this information aligns with the agenda of dark forces.

> *The "absence" of a nationality, as indicated by the [negro and black brands] created a "prima facie" social status; and the eventual established fact of the demanded public declaration of their "Moorish Nationality" made the difference in their "Legal Status" in Law, in North American society. Negroes i.e., "branded" persons do not come under the secured protections of the Constitution. Negroes come under the authority and the jurisdiction of the "Negro Acts" and under other "Black Codes" dictums.[4]*

The Holy Prophet warned "I love my people and I desire their unity and mine back to their own free national and divine standards because day by day, they have been violating the national and constitutional laws of their government by claiming names and principles that are unconstitutional. If Italians, Greeks, English, Chinese, Japanese, Turks, and Arabians are forced to proclaim their free national name and religion before the constitutional government of the United States of America, it is no more than right that the law should be enforced upon all other American citizens alike." ~Noble Drew Ali

Now let's look at identity.

IDENTITY Definition & Legal Meaning Definition & Citations: In the law of evidence. Sameness; the fact that a subject, person, or thing before a court is the same as it is represented, claimed, or charged to be.[5]

---

4. 1. Taj Tarik Bey, "Moors of the Round Table 6 Week Civics Class - Class 2" (R.V. Bey Publications, n.d.).
5. "Identity," in *The Law Dictionary*.

By applying common sense and examining the lawful definition of identity, the facts should be self-explanatory. Once again, facts are not up for debate; they stand on their own merits. Choosing to disregard the truth doesn't alter its fundamental nature. This reality can be a tough pill to swallow for many, given the constant 24/7 operation of social engineering.

The word "claim" is rooted in the term "proclaim." Preceded by the prefix "pro," which originates from Latin, meaning "forward," "bring into existence," "before," or "outside of" (as in "profane"), it is also of Latin origin. The "pro" prefix signifies strong support and is the opposite of the prefix "anti." Additionally, "pro" forms words denoting forward movement or status, such as "proceed," "progress," "advancement," "promote," and "propose." In the context of "claim," it means to demand by or as if by virtue of a right, to assert or maintain as a fact, for example, claiming an estate by inheritance.

> ***Claim*** *to demand as one's own or as one right; To assert; To urge; To assist. A cause of action.* [6]

> ***Proclamation*** *that is the act of publicly proclaiming; A formal declaration, giving notice of a governmental act that has been done or is to be done. The act of causing some governmental matters to be published or made generally known.* [7]

The United States has established laws enabling individuals who acquire nationality after birth to claim the rights and privileges of U.S. Citizenship (8 U.S.C.A. § 1401 et seq.). Additionally, treaties hold the highest legal authority within the country, particularly in cases where specific groups are granted citizenship (e.g., the Louisiana Purchase) or through Congressional laws for the annexation of entire territories, like Texas, Hawaii, Alaska, and others.

---

6. Henry C. Black, "Claim," in *Black's Law Dictionary* (St. Paul, MN: West Publishing, 1951).
7. Ibid, "Proclaim."

What's intriguing is that so-called "Blacks" are often unaware of why they are exempt from the scrutiny of the U.S. Department of Immigration and Naturalization Service, or why they are systematically excluded from the rigorous processes of nationality that apply to other groups. They may wonder why other nations have formal "Naturalization Ceremonies," while they do not.

> Nations of the earth recognize and honor the name of a former national, far more than its military might. When one proclaims, I am Chinese, one has given a wealth of information and a mindful of heritage in a single expression. China's military or economic structure, etc are preceded by the free national name, Chinese which matches the landmass called China. [8]

In essence, terms like "negro," "black," and "colored" have been used in the quest for recognition without providing a free and authentic name for a particular group of people. Consider the act of proclaiming a nationality as donning national and international protective armor, shielding against genocide, mistreatment, and abuses.

## Identifying the cobwebs

"Immigratin Tsunami"
Original Artist:CNSNews.com

The ongoing conflict between Moors and Europeans revolves around the theft of birthrights. To a Moor, all Europeans are considered foreign entities and jurisdictions. The Constitution for the Republic stands as the established Supreme Law of the land. A significant element of propaganda and fraudulent narrative revolves around the misconception that America was founded as a democracy. In reality, nothing could be farther from the truth. This

---

8. Elihu N. Pleasant-Bey, *Noble Drew Ali, the Last Prophet: The Exhuming of a Nation* (Seven Seals Publication, 2009), 224-225.

deception becomes evident when one recites the pledge of allegiance; the fallacy of the so-called "democracy" is glaringly apparent in the lyrics.

> "I pledge allegiance to the flag of the United States of America and to the REPUBLIC for which it STANDS one NATION under God indivisible for LIBERTY AND JUSTICE FOR ALL."

The word democracy is not mentioned one time in the entire Constitution. Just let that sink in...

### Keys to analyze:

Article 4 sec 4. of the United States Constitution states as follows:

The Guarantee Clause

Article IV, Section 4 is generally known as the Guarantee Clause. 1 Through its terms, the United States makes three related assurances to the states: (1) a guarantee of a republican form of government; (2) protection against foreign invasion; and (3) upon request by the state, protection against internal insurrection or rebellion.

### What is the difference between a Democracy and a Republic??

Democracy is a system of governance by the masses. Authority is established through mass meetings or any form of direct expression, leading to decisions based on collective accuracy. The approach to property is communistic, which negates individual property rights. Regarding law, it dictates that the will of the majority should prevail, whether it arises from careful deliberation or is influenced by passion, prejudice, and impulse, without limitations or consideration for consequences. This often results in demagoguery, a lack of restraint, agitation, discontent, and even anarchy.

In contrast, a Republic is a system where authority is derived from the election of public officials by the people, chosen for their ability to best represent them. This system upholds respect for laws and individual rights, and follows a sensible economic procedure. It regards the administration of justice as conforming to established principles and supported by solid evidence, with strict attention to consequences. A Republic can encompass a larger number of citizens and a broader expanse of territory. It steers clear of the dangerous extremes of either tyranny or mob rule. The outcomes are statesmanship, liberty, reason, justice, contentment, and progress.

## The United States Exists In Two Forms

The United States exists in two forms: the original united States, which governed the federal system until 1860, and the federal United States, which was incorporated in 1871. The government of the original united States of America was supplanted by the government of the federal United States, which solely exercises authority over the District of Columbia and its territories (Washington, D.C.). It operates as a for-profit corporation, functioning as our National Government, under public commercial law rather than private common law.

The original Constitution and the Declaration of Independence refer to "these united States." Here, "united" is an adjective modifying the noun "States," hence the lowercase "united." However, when the federal United States was established in 1871, the adjective "united" was changed to the noun "United," as the federal "United States" is a corporation, making it a noun rather than an adjective.

The Constitution of the original united States of America was never abolished; it has remained dormant since 1871 and is still in effect to this day. This fact was underscored by Supreme Court Justice Marshall Harlan in the case of <u>Downes v. Bidwell</u> (182 U.S. 244, 1901) through his dissenting opinion: "Two national governments exist; one to be maintained under the Constitution with all its restrictions; the other to be maintained by Congress outside and independently of that Instrument."

The revised 1871 Constitution of the United States (Inc.) takes precedence over the original Constitution for the united States of America. This accounts for why our Congressmen and Senators do not adhere to it, and why the President (CEO) of the Corporate United States can issue Executive Orders at will. He operates under corporate laws that effectively strip sovereign individuals of their God-given unalienable rights.

> *Corporate public commercial law is not sovereign (private), for it is public agreement between two or more parties under public contract.*
>
> *Common law (under which sovereigns operate) is not commercial law; common law and private.*[9]

One of our problems is that when we engage with government, municipalities and other such elements, and all our dealings in the law when we have been conditioned to interact on and in their level. We as a nation have never risen to the level where the base of law is, where the reality, the power, the solidity and the preeminence exists-the Sovereign's level. But now, we can function on this powerful level. This is checkmate.

### What is treason?

The offense or attempting by overt acts to overthrow the government of the state to which the offender owes allegiance; or of betraying the state into the hands of a foreign power. Treason consists of two elements: adherence to the enemy, and rendering him aid and comfort. Treason against the united states shall consist only in levying war against them, or in adhering to their enemies.[10]

---

9. David E. Robinson, *Common Law Handbook: For Juror's, Sheriff's, Bailiff's, and Justice's* (CreateSpace, 2013).

10. U.S. Const., art. 3 § 3, clause 1

*Misprision of treason*

1. A contempt against the sovereign, the government, or the courts of justice, including not only contempts of court, properly so-called, but also all forms of seditious or disloyal conduct leze-majesty.

2. Maladministration of high public office, including peculation of the public funds;

3. A neglect or light account made of a crime, that is, failure in the duty of a citizen to endeavor to prevent the Commission of a crime, or a comma having knowledge of its Commission, to reveal it to the proper authorities; And the concealment of something which ought to be revealed.

4. Neglect or light account made of a crime, that is, failure in the duty of a citizen to endeavor to prevent the Commission of a crime, or, having knowledge of its Commission, to reveal it to the proper authorities; And the concealment of something which ought to be revealed.[11]

## What is fraud?

"An intentional perversion of truth for the purpose of inducing another in reliance upon it to part with some valuable thing belonging to him, or to surrender a legal right"; a false representation of a matter of fact, whether by words or by conduct; By false or misleading allegations, or by concealment of that which should been disclosed, which deceives "and is intended to deceive another, so that he shall act upon it to his legal injury." Fraud is a generic term, embracing all multifarious means with human ingenuity can devise, and which are resorted to by one individual to get the advantage over another by false suggestions or by suppression of truth and includes all surprise, trick, and cunning, dissembling, and any other unfair way to which another is cheated. Bad faith and fraud are synonymous, and also synonymous of dishonesty, infidelity, faithfulness, perfidy, unfairness, ETC., and consist

---

11. Black, "Treason," in *Black's Law Dictionary*

of some deceitful practice or willful device, resorted to with the "intent to deprive another of his right, or in some manner to do him an injury. As distinguished from negligence it is always intentional."[12]

### Reconstructed Propaganda

The Republican Party in each southern state rested on the basis of the negro voter.[13]

Republican power in the South depended on 3 supports: The Negro vote, republican control of the national government and particularly of the presidency, and the presence of federal troops in the South.[14]

Reconstruction was the transforming changes that occurred in the entire nation between 1865 and 1877 the year when southern "whites" overthrew the last republican state governments in their section and ended political reconstruction.[15]

All attempts of the rich whites to dominate the Negro failed, and finally the promoters joined the general white opposition to radical reconstruction.[16]

By one method or another, legal or illegal, every white man was to be forced to join the Democratic Party or leave the community by similar methods, every Negro male was to be excluded from political action; in a few states he was permitted to vote-if he voted Democratic.[17]

Lincoln's proclamation asked the South to recognize the reality that slavery was dead but it did not require that a state formally abolished slavery as an institution.[18]

The black holes were the Southern solution for the problem of the Negro laborer and its substitute for slavery as a white supremacy device.[19]

---

12. Black, "Fraud," in *Black's Law Dictionary*
13. T. Harry Williams, Richard N. Current, and Frank Freidel, *A History of the United States [to 1877]*, 2nd ed. (Alfred A. Knopf, 1965),23.
14. Ibid, 25.
15. Ibid, 7.
16. Ibid, 24.
17. Ibid, 28.
18. Ibid, 12.
19. Ibid, 6.

> Some states passed their laws for the specific purpose of forcing the negroes back to the plantations and farms. Socially the codes were designed to govern relations between the races to define the position of the former slaves in the southern society, and invest the negroes with a recognized and legal although subordinate status.[20]

Those who believed that education and economic progress were insufficient and advocated for more militant approaches formed a loosely organized group called "The Niagara Movement." However, in 1909, following a race riot in Springfield, Illinois, they united to create the National Association for the Advancement of Colored People [N.A.A.C.P.]. While most of the new society's officials were white, the driving force behind it was W.E.B. Du Bois.

---

20. Ibid, 16.

# End Notes

Black, Henry C. "Claim." In *Black's Law Dictionary*. St. Paul, MN: West Publishing, 1951.

———. "Fraud." In *Black's Law Dictionary*. St. Paul, MN: West Publishing, 1951.

———. "Treason." In *Black's Law Dictionary*. St. Paul, MN: West Publishing, 1951.

"Faith Definition & Meaning | *Dictionary.Com*." In Dictionary.Com, September 16, 2020. https://www.dictionary.com/browse/faiths.

"Identity." In *The Law Dictionary*, November 9, 2011. Accessed June 6, 2023. https://thelawdictionary.org/identity.

"Nationality." In *The Law Dictionary*, November 9, 2011. Accessed June 6, 2023. https://thelawdictionary.org/identity.

Pleasant-Bey, Elihu N. *Noble Drew Ali, the Last Prophet: The Exhuming of a Nation*. Seven Seals Publication, 2009.

Robinson, David E. *Common Law Handbook: For Juror's, Sheriff's, Bailiff's, and Justice's*. CreateSpace, 2013.

U.S. Constitution, art.III, § 3, clause 1.

Williams, T. Harry, Richard N. Current, and Frank Freidel. *A History of the United States [to 1877]*. 2nd ed. Alfred A. Knopf, 1965.

# Chapter 6

## U.S CORPORATION

Federal agency or agency = government corporation, government controlled corporation, any other establishment in the executive branch (including the Executive Office of the President), or any independent regulatory agency

The distinction between the organic American soil for "We the People" and the U.S. CORPORATION must be clearly conveyed to the reader and understood.

The UNITED STATES INC consists only of the ten miles square of Washington, D.C and its territories of Guam, Samoa, Mariana Islands, and Puerto Rico etc.

Plenary Power: One of the powers granted to Congress in the federal Constitution is outlined in Article 1, Section 8, Clauses 16 and 17.

> 16. to exercise exclusive legislation in all cases whatsoever, over such district not exceeding 10 mile square as made, by session of particular states, and the acceptance of Congress, become the seat of government of the United states, and to exercise like authority over all places purchased, by the consent of the legislature of the state in which the same shall be, for the erection of forts, magazines, arsenals, dockyards, and the needful buildings: and

> 17. to make all laws which shall be necessary and proper for carrying into execution the foregoing powers, and all the new powers vested by this constitution and the government of the United states, or in any department or officer thereof.[1]

Congress possesses absolute—or what is described as plenary—power, including police power and similar authorities. Where does Congress have such plenary power? Only within the geographical area of the District of Columbia, and all forts, magazines, arsenals,

---

1. U.S. Const., art. I, §§ 16-17.

dockyards, and other needful buildings within the several states.

The UNITED STATES exists only on paper. It is a total fiction. It exists only as an idea, whereas the various state republics of the union exist in substance and reality. The United States takes on a physical reality only after Congress activates 18 constitutionally delegated powers in accordance with article 1, section seven of the U.S. Constitution.[2] Article one, Section 8, clauses 16 and 17 set this out: The U.S. Congress has the right to make laws only regarding Washington DC – within its 10 square miles – and the other territories owned by the United states. This limited scope of legislative powers is its only lawful authority relative to the people of the various states... meaning anything connected or pertaining to the U.S. CORPORATION has ZERO AUTHORITY over the organic, aboriginal, indigenous, various copper-complexioned Moorish people. None at all.

The U.S CORPORATION has only been able to function because the people have been unwittingly participating in the fraud. Who would have thought it could be that simple and hidden in plain sight? Going back to the Constitution let's look at Article 6 of Constitution of the United States

### Article VI

*All Debts contracted and Engagements entered into, before the Adoption of this Constitution, shall be as valid against the United States under this Constitution, as under the Confederation.*

*This Constitution, and the Laws of the United States which shall be made in Pursuance thereof; and all Treaties made, or which shall be made, under the Authority of the United States, shall be the supreme Law of the Land; and the Judges in every State shall be bound thereby, any Thing in the Constitution or Laws of any State to the Contrary notwithstanding.*

---

2. David E. Robinson, *New Beginning Study Course: Connect the Dots and See!* (CreateSpace, 2009), 42-43.

> *The Senators and Representatives before mentioned, and the Members of the several State Legislatures, and all executive and judicial Officers, both of the United States and of the several States, shall be bound by Oath or Affirmation, to support this Constitution; but no religious Test shall ever be required as a Qualification to any Office or public Trust under the United States.[3]*

Did you catch that? All debts and engagements entered into BEFORE this Constitution and every state is BOUND THEREBY, any thing in the Constitution or Laws of any State to the CONTRARY notwithstanding. It also mentioned all treaties made. So, let's examine the Barbary Treaties of 1786-1836 between the US and the Barbary State, the Treaty of Peace and Friendship of 1786-1836 between Morocco and the US, and House Joint Resolution 75.

These treaties affirm the presence of a Muhammadan nation in America, formerly known as al Morocco or the Northgate. This country was not established on Christianity, as stated in Article 11 of the Treaty of Tripoli: "As for the Government of the United States of America, it is not, in any sense, founded on the Christian religion; as it has in itself no character of enmity against the laws, religion, or tranquility of Muslims, and as the said States never entered into any war or act of hostility against any Mohammedan nation, it is declared that no pretext arising from religious opinions shall ever produce an interruption of the harmony existing between the two nations."

The Constitution draws from Moslem (Moorish Law), which is why it may not be emphasized or taught extensively in the school systems. It was designed to maintain a system of checks and balances, with the intention of keeping the so-called government in check, not the other way around.

---

3. U.S. Const., art. VI.

> **1933 - LEGISLATIVE JOURNAL - HOUSE - PAGE 5759**
> **RESOLUTION No. 75**
>
> Mr. WITKIN, Mr. Speaker, I desire at this time to call up Resolution No. 75, Printer's No. 1034.
>
> **The Resolution was read by the Clerk as follows:**
>
> In the House of Representatives, April 17, 1933. Many sons and daughters of that proud and handsome race which inspired the architecture of Northern Africa and carried
> into Spain the influence of its artistic temperaments have become citizens of this Nation.
> In the City of Philadelphia there exists a Moorish-American Society made up of Moors who have found here the end of their quest for a home and of the children of those who journeyed here from the plains of Morocco.
>
> This Society has done much to bring about a thorough absorption by these people of those principles which are necessary to make them good American citizens. These Moorish-Americans have since being here missed the use of the titles and name annexations that were so familiar at home and which are used in accordance with the doctrines of the religious faith to which they are adherents therefore be it, Resolved That this House commends the Moorish-American Society of Philadelphia for the efficient service it has rendered the Nation in bringing about a speedy and thorough Americanization of these former Moors and that in accordance with the fullest right of religious independence guaranteed every citizen we recognize also the right of these people to use the name affixes El or Ali or Bey or any other prefix or suffix to which they have heretofore been accustomed to use or which they may hereafter acquire the right to use.
>
> On the question, **Will the House Adopt the resolution?**
>
> **It was Adopted May 4, 1933**

*House Joint Resolution 75.*
*Scribd.com*

Noble Drew Ali instructed Moorish Americans to actively enforce the Constitution, emphasizing his preference for [pro]active Moors over passive ones. The most crucial and fundamentally necessary task lies in upholding the United States Republic Constitution, wherein our rights to life, liberty, and the pursuit of happiness are safeguarded. We are not to enforce state codes, statutes, ordinances, or executive orders. Why? Because they do not and cannot apply to Samaritans. Codes, statutes, ordinances, and executive orders pertain to citizens of the union states, not to Moorish Americans. As affirmed in the original 13th article of the Bill of Rights, section 12, it's time to turn off the lights, and then come on, you know.

## The 13th, 14th Amendments

*"The traffic in slaves with African is hereby forever prohibited on pain of death and the forfeiture of all the rights and property of persons engaged therein; And the descendants of Africans shall not be citizens."* [4]

The 13th Amendment explicitly states, "neither slavery nor involuntary servitude." These are strict prohibitions, leaving no room for alternative interpretations. It does not address voluntary servitude, as that remains an individual's choice. If you willingly enter a contract of involuntary servitude, that decision is yours to make.

Following immediately after the 13th Amendment, the 14th Amendment introduces the concept of being "born or naturalized and subject to the jurisdiction." When filling out forms, there is often a question about whether you are a citizen of the United States and subject to its jurisdiction. Here, "jurisdiction" is a modern term akin to allegiance, which, in feudal terms, implies a relationship to the land or the liege.

So, are you under the jurisdiction of the United States both as a citizen of the United States and of the state in which you reside? It's crucial to note that "residence" in a state does not equate to citizenship in that state; it typically pertains to commercial matters. Therefore, on government and job applications, among others, they inquire about U.S. citizenship and request a residence address.

When you combine being a citizen of the United States with being a resident in a state, you essentially volunteer to be treated as a second-class citizen, regarded as property of the United States. It's important to recognize that when the term "United States" is used, it refers to the corporations.

---

4. U.S. Const., amend 13.

Ch.6

The 14th Amendment introduced some confusion regarding the fundamental understanding of one's legal status because it established a new category of citizen: United States citizens, which did not exist previously. The newly emancipated individuals, often referred to as "black citizens," had little knowledge of the Constitution, let alone the government's jurisdiction over distinct classes of individuals prior to its adoption. Citizens or individuals with state status were automatically considered citizens of the American empire. Nevertheless, state citizenship held precedence, and American citizenship derived from state citizenship.

Before the 14th Amendment in 1868, there were no individuals considered as being born or naturalized in the United States. Naturalization was managed at the state level, with each person being born or naturalized in one of the several states. Following the Civil War, a new class of citizen was established. This marked the commencement of the shift away from the Republic and the establishment of a United States democracy, with its epicenter being the District of Columbia. The American people in the Republic, within the various Republic states, could opt for the advantages of federal citizenship, similar to one of the new United States citizens, if they so wished.[5]

> "The 14th and 15th amendments are not needed for the salvation of my people." ~ Noble Drew Ali

## What kind of person are you?

*Person: In general usage, a human being(i.e. natural person), though by statute term may include labor organizations, partnerships, associations, corporations, legal representatives, trustees, trustees in bankruptcy, or receivers."*[6]

---

5. Melvin Stamper JD, *Fruit from a Poisonous Tree* (iUniverse, 2008).
6. Henry Campbell Black, "Person," in *Black's Law Dictionary* (Springer, May 31, 1992).

Notice that there are two types of person described:

1. A human being (natural person with natural rights) i.e. Nationals.

2. May include (artificial entities or legal fictions with legal rights) COLORED PERSONS

## What is a Natural Person?

A natural person is an actual human being, which is different from an "artificial person," which is a distinction under the law to establish whether a person is acting or appearing as himself, acting or appearing on behalf of a business or other entity. This is because a legal or artificial person is not a person at all, but is instead a collective of people that is being considered as one single entity for the purposes of a legal action. For example, a natural person is different from a legal person, which might be a company, a trust, a partnership, or some other group.

> Noun
> 1. An individual human being, with consciousness of self
> 2. A human being, as opposed to a "legal" person, which is an entity or group considered collectively as a single individual for legal purposes.
>
> Origin: 1175-1225 Latin persōna i[7]

Following is a list of the individual characteristics of natural and legal persons:

Natural Person

- A human being; a real and living person.

- Possessing the power of thought and choice.

- May also be a legal person, and perform the organization's functions.

- Lives for a limited period, meaning he or she will die at some point.

---

7. Ibid, "Natural Person."

### What is an artificial person?

Yet another difference between a natural person and a legal person is that a natural person can only be classified as a living, breathing human being. The legal person definition can be used to refer to a host of organizations. For example, natural persons differ from legal persons in that the latter consist of deceased persons, unborn persons, partnerships, corporations, universities, societies, and companies, to name a few. Legal persons can also be referred to as "fictitious," "artificial," or "moral" persons.

Legal Person

- A being, real or imaginary, created by the law, or which the law regards as capable of certain rights or duties

- Also referred to as "fictitious," "juristic," "artificial" or "moral"

- Includes deceased persons, corporations, companies, trusts, and other organizations

- Can only perform their functions through natural persons

- Does not die, but may be disbanded or done away with.

### Differences Between Natural Living Beings and Legal Persons

There are distinct differences between a natural person and a legal person. To begin, a natural person is an actual living human being with a unique personality. They generally possess the ability to think independently and make personal decisions, though a person who lacks competence in decision-making still falls under the category of a natural person.

In the eyes of the law, a legal person is an entity endowed with certain rights and privileges. Although not a human being, it is granted the capacity to assert legal claims or bear legal responsibilities. For example, a partnership or a corporation is recognized as a legal person for legal proceedings. Additionally, a natural person can also take on the role of a legal person and perform both functions. However, it's important to note that a legal person can only exercise its functions through natural persons.

Another significant distinction between a natural person and a legal person is their lifespan. Typically, a natural person's life does not extend much beyond a century. Conversely, a legal person, such as a corporation, can persist beyond the lifespan of any individual involved. It can be passed down to successors of its president or continue to benefit generations through a trust. The corporation or trust can continue its operations long after its founder has passed away.

The name of the game between Moors and Europeans is always
**BIRTH RIGHT THEFT.**

*"In common usage, the term "person" does not include the Sovereign, statues employing the word person are ordinarily construed to exclude the Sovereign."* <u>Wilson v. Omaha Tribe</u>, 442 U.S. 653, 667 (1979); <u>United States v. Cooper Corp.</u>, 312 600, 604 (1941).[8]

*"Ignorance is of the law no excuse."* ~ Maxim of Law

*"Ignorance of the law does not excuse misconduct in anyone, least of all in a sworn officer of the law."* <u>McCowan (1917), 177 C. 93 170</u> pg. 1100.

As a Moor, it is your duty to step forward and uphold the United States Republic Constitution, ensuring that the Supreme Law of the Land is followed. This applies not only to foreign Europeans but also to the Moors of North Amexem, or North America.

One of the key tactics employed has been to coax the original indigenous inhabitants of this land into relinquishing their inherent rights through deceit. It's crucial to recognize this linguistic <u>manipulation in</u> order to steer clear of potential pitfalls.

8. "Dissertation of Property," R. V. Bey Publications, accessed July 8, 2023, http://rvbeypublications.com/.

It's essential to understand that a deceased entity, legally termed a "legal person" or "legal fiction," possesses no inherent rights; it is endowed only with artificial rights and privileges. For instance, a United States citizen is considered a legal person, governed solely by artificial rights and privileges in the eyes of the legal system. This is why, when you (as a United States citizen) assert your natural or constitutional rights in court, the judge may regard you with bewilderment and possibly instruct you to remain seated and quiet. If you persist in speaking out, you may be charged with contempt of court.

Because a legal person (e.g., a United States citizen) is considered a lifeless entity, the government holds jurisdiction over it. Conversely, a living and breathing individual is not deceased and, as such, possesses natural rights bestowed upon them by God. The term "unalienable" signifies that these rights cannot be relinquished, sold, or transferred. According to A Dictionary of Law (1889), an unalienable right is defined as one that "cannot be surrendered to government or society, because no equivalent can be received for it, and one which neither the government nor society can take away, conscience." In simpler terms, your natural rights (unalienable rights) stand above all government-made "laws"; they cannot be traded or surrendered. Consequently, the government lacks jurisdiction over you, the living individual. However, if you inflict harm upon another individual or violate their natural rights, they have the right to seek government intervention to administer justice. [9]

When you encounter terms like "person," "straw man," "minority," or "legal entity," they all essentially refer to an artificial person. Let's now consider a different viewpoint on ignorance, drawing from Lobsang Rampa's book, "Wisdom of the Ancients:"

> *Ignorance: Ignorance is lack of knowledge, lack of wisdom, and if we were not so foolishly ignorant we should not have so many troubles.*

---

9. Pao Chang, *Word Magic: The Powers and Occult* Definitions of Words (Second Edition) (Esoteric Knowledge Publishing, 2019), 37-38.

> The ignorant person does not know enough to know that he does not know. Perhaps the best way to explain it is:
>
> He that knows not and knows not that he knows not, he is a fool, shun him.
>
> He that knows not and knows that he knows not, he is teachable, teach him.
>
> He that knows and knows that he knows, he is wise, follow him.
>
> Ignorance causes confusion, doubt and fear. Which in turn causes chaos, disharmony and disorder. [10]

## Nation Building

Nationhood is the only means by which modern civilization can completely protect itself.

Let's take a look at what Noble Drew Ali says in his literature in the National Mission Statement.

> The advent of we, the Moorish Americans, was divinely ordained forth into rightful existence, in due time as a nation, by the will of the great God at the abolishment of slavery, as ratified by the United states congressional 13th amendment in 1865 AD. This congressional manumission of the sons and daughters of Africa brought to light a new nation of people upon the earth. This new nation of West African descendants has now come to lawfully link themselves again with the families of nations and to worship under their own vine and fig tree, which have been the inherited birthrights of all men through the descendant nature of their ancient forefathers. This is the true and inalienable inheritance to every member of the human family and nation upon the earth. And the Moorish Americans are part and parcel of the human family.

Now let's take a look at what Marcus Garvey says about Nation building:

---

10. T. Lobsang Rampa, *Wisdom of the Ancients* (Important Books, 2013).

*Independence of nationality, independence of government, is the means of protecting not only the individual, but the group.*

*Nationhood is the highest ideal of all peoples.*

*The evolutionary scale that weighs nations and races, balances alike for all peoples; hence we feel sure that someday the balance will register a change for the Negro.*

*If we are to believe the divine injunction, we must realize that the time is coming when every man and every race must return to its own "vine and fig tree".*

## Booby traps

What is a tribe?

*tribe. n. A socially, ethnically, and politically cohesive group of people. tribe noun A society larger than a band but smaller than a state; n. The collective noun for various animals; n. A hierarchal rank between family and genus.*[11]

Tribes, tribes, tribes. They are advertised heavily within the so called black, Indian persons of color community. When someone say's "I'm part of a tribe," it has to be known that tribes do not identify a nationality. The United Nations Declaration Rights of Indigenous Peoples has NO MENTION of the Indian, Hebrew, Native American, Latino, West Indian, people of color, minorities, etc.

*"Every indigenous individual has the right to a nationality."* [12]

This information is readily available, but as you can see, it's not taught to Moorish people because ignorance is a trillion-dollar industry. This deceptive trap has been devastating to the Moorish people of the Americas for generations. Nationality is more than just a legal status; it's your bloodline, connecting you to history, land, culture, laws,

---

11. "Tribe," Definitions.net, n.d., https://www.definitions.net/definition/Tribe.

12. United Nations General Assembly, "Declaration on the Rights of Indigenous Peoples," 61st plenary meeting, UN Doc. A/RES/61/295 (13 September 2007) art. 6.

customs, traditions, and morals. To be stripped of your nationality is to lose your connection to all these vital aspects. The term "tribe" is essentially synonymous with "family." These mini-tribes, when united, form the foundation of a nation. It's important to note that a family name isn't the same as the name of the nation itself. The tribal name serves as a distinctive, traditional identifier for families with similar yet distinct cultural practices, ceremonies, appearance, or even specific geographic locations within the natural borders of the nation. For instance, a family near a river might be distinguished from another tribe on the opposite side of the river closer to the mountains. Despite these differences, they are still unified by shared culture, language, traditions, trade, and resources. Together, these tribes collectively comprise the nation, rather than existing as independent entities.

## Examples of Tribes:

*Guyana*
*CarribeanCricket / Flickr.com*

*Trinadad and Tobaygo*
*C. Young / Outlish.com*

*Cuba*
*Workers.org*

*Bahamas*
*F. Martinez / TheWichitan.com*

*Haiti*
Z. DeClerck / PartnersInHealth.com

*Belize*
A Beach Bum Retires in Belize / WesternBelizeHappenings.com

*Guatemala*
Source: M. Castillo / A.P.

*Chile*
Source: N. Reyes-Escobar / Wikipedia.org

*Bolivia*
U. Marcelino / CatholicSpirit.com

*Venezuela*
El Nuevo Herald / Maduradas.com

The antidote to tribalism lies in embracing nationalism. The nation serves as an individual's broad political "umbrella," surpassing the social protection provided by the tribe to its members. Tribalism poses a threat to nationalism because loyalty to one's tribe can undermine one's allegiance to the nation, thriving at its expense. Similarly, familial loyalty can sometimes overshadow tribal allegiance, weakening it. Therefore, maintaining loyalty to the nation is crucial.

The relationship between a nation and the global community mirrors that of a family and a tribe. The more internal strife and fanaticism within a tribe, the greater the threat to the tribe as a whole. Likewise, a family is jeopardized when individual members solely pursue their personal interests. In a parallel vein, if the tribes within a nation quarrel and prioritize their own interests, it undermines the nation.

A progressive, productive, and civilized nation benefits not only itself but the entire world. However, when the national political structure stoops to a lower social level, emulating the family and tribe, and adopts their perspectives, it incurs damage.

The nation represents an expanded family that has evolved beyond the tribal stage and diversified into various tribes, all stemming from a common origin. It is a social entity united by nationalism. In contrast, the tribe is a social structure bound by tribalism, the family by familial ties, and global society by our shared humanity. These truths are self-evident.

When the political structure aligns with social reality, as seen in the case of the nation-state, it endures and remains stable. When each nation clings firmly to its national identity, it seeks independence, causing political empires to dissolve as their constituents revert to their social roots. This pattern is clearly evident when examining world history throughout the ages.

Why were those empires comprised of diverse nations? The answer lies in understanding that the state is not a social structure like the family, tribe, or nation. Rather, it's a political entity formed by various factors, with nationalism being the most fundamental. The national state is the sole political form that aligns with the natural social order. Its endurance persists, unless it succumbs to the dominance of a stronger nationalism or unless its political structure is influenced by its social makeup, including tribes, clans, and families. A political structure falters when it becomes subservient to the sectarian social order of the family, tribe, or sect and adopts their characteristics. Religious, economic, and military factors also contribute to shaping a state that deviates from the foundational, national state.

The foundation of individual life is the family, extending to the tribe, nation, and ultimately, all of humanity. The pivotal factor remains social: nationalism is a perpetual force. Emphasis should be placed on acknowledging social reality and providing familial support to nurture a well-rounded, educated individual.

Next, attention should be given to the tribe as a social "umbrella" and a natural social institution that cultivates its members after the family stage. The nation comes after. Individuals primarily imbibe social values from the family and the tribe, constituting a natural social structure not created by any specific individual. Caring for the family is in the individual's best interest, just as the welfare of the tribe is in the interest of the family, the individual, and the nation; it is integral to national identity. The social factor, the national factor, serves as the enduring, dynamic force driving history.

Disregarding the national bond of human communities and establishing a political system in opposition to social reality only erects a transient structure, susceptible to crumbling under the influence of the social factor within those groups — that is, the national cohesion and vitality of each community.

These truths are ingrained in human life and are not mere intellectual conjectures. Every individual worldwide should be cognizant of these realities and act accordingly, ensuring their actions hold value. To prevent deviation, disorder, and harm in the lives of human groups — outcomes resulting from a lack of comprehension and respect for these principles of human life — it is imperative to recognize these proven truths.[13]

---

13. Muammar Al-Gaddafi, *Gaddafi's the Green Book* (Createspace Independent Publishing Platform, 2016), 79-83.

*National Flag of the Moorish Nation*

The national flag of the Moabite Moorish Nation of North America proudly displays a vibrant cherry red background with a prominent five-pointed green star at its center. This distinctive flag stands as a powerful emblem of the Moorish Nation's identity. The Moabite Nation established a Republican form of government, distinctly different from a "DEMOCRACY," a system which was suppressed and overthrown in 1861-1871 under an Act of Congress. The red and green colors hold a direct connection to the so-called Christmas season.

Ever wonder about the star atop the Christmas tree? The continental flag, symbolizing the continents, features a pine tree or evergreen, representing the concept of everlasting life. It all ties back. When George Washington claimed, "I chopped down the cherry tree," he was essentially celebrating the dismantling of Moorish rights and nationality.

*Continental Flag of the Moorish Nation*

*Banner of the united states of America*

The banner representing the colonial states of the union, reflecting the English, Irish, Germans, French, Scottish, and Dutch Holland companies/corporations/guilds, is characterized by seven red stripes and six white stripes, totaling 13. Additionally, it includes a blue canton with white stars, symbolizing the states. This design was officially adopted in 1932.

George Washington, who served as the chairman of the Continental Congress in 1774, is documented as having said, "If we would agree to take the fezes and turbans off the Moors' heads, remove the sandals from their feet, and enforce it with severe punishments, and also swear a death oath amongst ourselves to religiously and faithfully prevent anyone from teaching Moorish children about their true heritage or ancestry. Instead, only allow them to be taught that they were truly Negroes, black people, and colored folks." Washington went on to predict that 200 years later, Moorish people would have no knowledge of their nationality, their forefathers' national name, or the land from which their ancestors hailed.

It's worth noting that George Washington, in addition to being a slave owner, was not the first president of the Republic, which remains a significant legal point. He wasn't even elected; he was appointed as the first president of what would soon become the U.S. CORPORATION. Once appointed, George had intentions to convert all the districts of the American lands that the Moors allowed them to reside on into states.

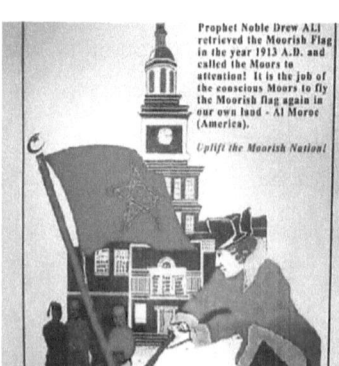

*George Washington Chopping Down the "Cherry Tree."*
*Taj Tariq Bey / Civic Lessons #1*

# End Notes

Al-Gaddafi, Muammar. *Gaddafi's the Green Book*. Createspace Independent Publishing Platform, 2016.

Chang, Pao. *Word Magic: The Powers and Occult Definitions of Words* (Second Edition). Esoteric Knowledge Publishing, 2019.

Definitions.net. "Tribe," n.d. https://www.definitions.net/definition/Tribe.

R. V. Bey Publications. "Dissertation of Property." Accessed July 8, 2023.

Rampa, T. Lobsang. *Wisdom of the Ancients*. Important Books, 2013.

Robinson, *David E. New Beginning Study Course: Connect the Dots and See!* CreateSpace, 2009.

United Nations General Assembly. "Declaration on the Rights of Indigenous Peoples." 61st plenary meeting. UN Doc. A/RES/61/295. 13 September 2007.

U.S. Constitution, art. I, §§ 16-17.

U.S. Constitution, art. art. VI.

# Notes

# Chapter 7

## What Does Conversion Mean in Law?

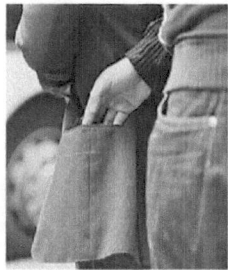

**Conversion**
/Con·ver·sion/ Noun
When someone takes your property for themselves or acts like something you own belongs to them

billgreen.law/glossary

## The basics of conversion.

Conversion occurs when one person appropriates — or converts — another person's property for their own use. Essentially, it's theft, plain and simple. Another perspective? It's when someone falsely claims ownership of something that rightfully belongs to someone else. Or, it's when someone alters or damages property in a way that affects its value, without the proper authority to do so because it isn't theirs to change.

Now let's look at the correlation of Moorish flags overseas — as you can see these flags are definitely of Moorish origin:

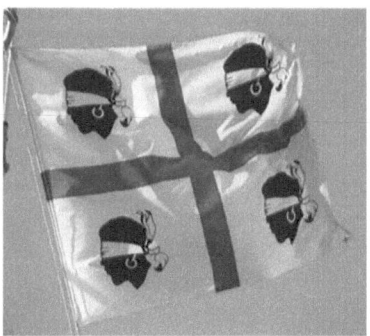

Blindfolded Moors – The Flags of Corsica and Sardinia.
ZiryabJamal / wisethedome.wordpress.com

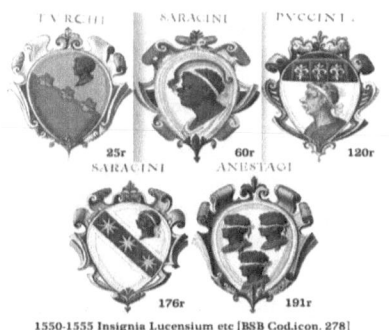

Black in European Art.
EgypSearch Forums

Pictures speak a thousand words. Moors are the original everything, especially in matters of royal families and bloodlines.

"Brotherhood of Blackheads." Royal Coat Of Arms with the signature Moorish horseshoe architecture.
Wikipedia Contributors,

## A Moorish-Irish Flag

The original Irish people were Moors. Yes!! Absolutely, without a doubt! The so-called Royals and the elite follow a different curriculum. They have the privilege of accessing rare and costly literature, whereas the mainstream education systems provide diluted versions of history. This is precisely why they maintain royal libraries and National Archives; they carry the true wealth of the Earth, which is wisdom, while the majority of humanity is led by a fabricated narrative.

https://www.amazon.com/stores/Irish+Rose+Gifts

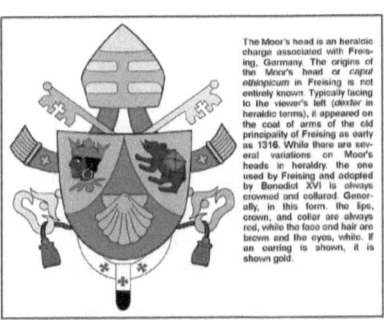

*The Papal crest of Pope Benedict E. Codfried / Blood Is Black Blood (1100-1848)*

*Pope Benedict XVI @ Mass, Yankee Stadium-New York Wiechec / CNS*

Look at the correlation.... Wow!!!!

You thought the Europeans invented something that Moors didn't do first? No! There's nothing new under sun.

## Moors and French, German, Dutch and Other European Families

Families on the misnomered European continent (Europe is part of Asia, not a separate continent) also incorporate Moors in their coat of arms, often in significant numbers. There are fifty or more variations of the word "Moor" across European languages.

*Mohrer Family Crest. RealHistoryWW.com*

*Brotherhood of the Blackheads (Riga, Latvia) / Nairaland.com*

*Queen-Consort Charlotte Sophia of England, Moorish German Princess, grandmother of Queen Victoria, 4th great-grandmother of current king, Charles III.*
*Attributed to A. Ramsay / Royal Collection Trust*

Moorish origin or with skin brown like that of a Moor, Mohr, der Mohr, Negar, Murel, Maurice, Maurand, Maurant, Maury, Maurian, Moreau, Moreaux, with these Moors and German nobility, the evident more restrained in queen Charlotte Sophia consort of George the third of England, who was a German Princess, might be explained.

In Holland and Germany, where names like swart, swarte, schwartz, schwarzmann, referring to what is commonly termed as black, exist, there are families bearing such names that incorporate individuals described as Negroes in their coats-of-arms. Belgium also boasts several Moers, de Moors, a Moor von Immersel, and other "Moors" with individuals referred to as Negroes. Some of these could have been individuals described as Negroes who served in the army of Spain during its rule over the Netherlands.

Statue of a Blackamoor holding a Habsburg Coat of Arms

*RealHistoryWW.com*

Poland features a Mora with a depiction of a Negro. In France, numerous families such as Moret, Morel, Moricaud, Morot, Moreau, and many other derivatives of Moor (Maure) are represented by individuals referred to as Negroes. Le Noir, a term still used in France for "the black man," was one of the prominent French families with branches in Anjou, Normandy, Brittany, and Beaune, and they too have a depiction of a so-called Negro. The Negre family, still utilized by the French to refer to individuals described as Negroes, also features a representation of a so-called Negro.

*Noble French Moor*

The saying goes: "If you wanna hide something from a black person, put it in a book." Phrases like that are not only dehumanizing but they underline a major problem that needs immediate correction hence the ancient saying "Seautom Gnothi" or "Know Thyself."

### What is "black face"?

White people darkened their faces not only for the Moorish dance but also out of an attraction to dark skin. Many British individuals with pale complexions used to artificially darken their faces so that they could more convincingly pass for Moors. To fully grasp this, one must shed all preconceived notions influenced by the American belief in color superiority.

However, one can discern a clear connection between this practice of darkening the skin, akin to that of the ancient Druids, and what many white individuals now seek to achieve through sun exposure, lotions, or tanning lamps. During one of Ben Johnson's masques held at Whitehall on January 12, 1605, Queen Anne of England and her ladies darkened their faces and arms up to the elbow.

Moorish lineage entered the English royal family. Even Elizabeth, the daughter of Edward IV and mother of Henry VIII, had several Moors in her family, including Count More and Count Morienne. Additionally, according to Turton, there is an Almoravit (Almoravide) that is unmistakably Moorish. The Almoravides were the conquerors of Spain in 1086 A.D., and they were described as "largely Negroes."

The lies have been perpetuated for generations, to the point where people may forget that Europeans initially adopted so-called blackface due to their fascination with a Moorish aesthetic, ironically enough. The media often tries to frame it as a matter of racism, though its origins have nothing to do with that.

*Zwarte Piets in The Hague, The Netherlands*
G. Stolk / GlobalVoices.org

This indoctrination of false information may provoke outrage when confronted with images like Zwarte Pete. Yet, in reality, it's a demonstration of how deeply European hybrids desire to emulate the appearance and style of Moors.

It's evident that so-called black and African American history constitutes an integral part of American history, and indeed, world history. Many of the elements mentioned wield significant influence over the world and afford safety and convenience to billions, save for a select few who hoard these resources. When these truths are exposed, they are often obscured by misnomers. This is partly why the inventors behind them were kept so well hidden. After all, fraud has no expiration date, rendering anything acquired through such means subject to confiscation and legal reclamation by the rightful heirs.

Consequently, one cannot conduct business in another person's name. The only genuine invention of colonizers was the patent, which served as their means to appropriate the ideas and hard work of true visionaries, stripping us of our titles and appellations in the process. It's not a matter of racism; it's birthright theft.

Schools can assert claim over the natural and political resources of their own land, as well as the territories, and jurisdictions belonging to their natural people. Unfortunately, naturalized citizens, subjects, and aliens have exploited the natural resources of indigenous and original peoples to the extent that it has led to the collapse and destruction of national economies. The universal solution is nationalization.[1]

> *What does not know self, does not know anything, but whoever knows self, already has acquired knowledge about the depths of the universe.*[2]

> *Question #16: How did the prophet begin to uplift the Moorish Americans? A. By teaching them to be themselves.*[3]

Moorish American children can only be taught how to be free and independent Moorish Americans by their Moorish American parents. Moorish children have a defined birthright to have their mind seasoned with the maxims of truth. It has been lies, falsehood and hypocrisy taught to the children of allah that has cast the world into present day chaos, war, famine and plagues of disease. Teach the children truth and the future of the world will be in peace.

Noble Drew Ali said to parents:

*Teach him obedience, and he shall bless thee.*

*Teach him modesty, and he shall not be ashamed.*

*Teach him gratitude, and he shall receive benefits period*

*Teach him charity, and he shall gain love.*

*Teach him temperance, and he shall have health.*

*Teach him prudence, and fortune shall attend him.*

---

1. Mishaal Talib Mahfuz El Bey, *The Torch: A Guide to S.E.L.F.* (Califa Media Publishing, 2020), 50-51.
2. Marvin Meyer, trans., *The Secret Teachings of Jesus: Four Gnostic Gospels* (Random House (NY), 1984).
3. T.S. Najee-Ullah El, ed., "Koran Questions for Moorish Americans:101s And Additional Laws," in *Califa Uhuru* (Califa Media Publishing, 2014), 141.

*Teach him justice, and he shall be honored by the world.*

*Teach him sincerity, and his own heart shall not reproach him.*

*Teach him diligence, and his wealth shall increase.*

*Teach him benevolence, and his mind shall be exalted.*

*Teach him science, and his life shall be useful.*

*Teach him religion, and his death shall be happy.*[4]

The breath of life, spirit, and soul signify that all children are fashioned from the essence of boundless perfection. This flawless seed ensures that the path of righteousness is ingrained in one's nature to become God. Armed with these advanced lessons in science, any parent can cultivate in their children their innate divinity. This, then, is the manner in which genuine Moorish Americans must pay tribute to their prophet: by adopting his and their own free national name. Without adherence to this law, members, Masons, and other NBC individuals should not anticipate different outcomes. For them, a more grievous fate is all but certain.

Doubt arises from fear, just as fear arises from ignorance. Those known as African-Americans need only to cultivate awareness of themselves, their God, and their history. When one lacks self-awareness, they are led without autonomy. Yet, with consciousness comes choice. The power of choice is synonymous with freedom. During the era of slavery, the Moors were deprived of this privilege. They were compelled to assume whatever label their slave masters imposed upon them, be it Negro, black, colored, African Americans, single moms, baby daddies, and so forth. Noble Drew Ali, having been divinely appointed, eventually delivered to his people the truth about themselves, their God, and their history - consciousness... and with it, choice.

---

4. "Holy Horan of the Moorish Science Temple of America Circle Seven." *Califa Uhuru*, ch.23, ver. 8-13.

## Race Pride

The reason why Moorish Americans haven't readily declared themselves as a distinct nation is due to their limited understanding of embracing race pride. Drew Ali instructed all Asiatics, "If you have race pride and love your race, come join the Moorish Science Temple and you will have the power to redeem your race."

What's intriguing about this document (pictured below) is that there were seven proclamations crafted in seven distinct cities, all endorsed by their respective mayors. These cities include:

- Atlanta, Georgia
- Chicago, Illinois
- Charlotte, North Carolina
- Baltimore, Maryland
- Fayetteville, North Carolina
- Lynchburg, Virginia
- Little Rock, Arkansas
- Trenton, New Jersey
- Tyler, Texas
- Omaha, Nebraska
- Tacoma, Washington.

Proclamations -
Image 49: Atlanta, Georgia January 2013
RVBeyPublications.com

There is no such thing as coincidence in all-law (Allah).

# A Moorish Parable

The Negro and the Sardine is a Moorish analogy. There are many species of small fish indigenous to the gray Seas of the earth and the great God did in fact create them all yet there is not one fish in any of the seas named sardine listen these as special fish are not labeled sardines until captured processed and canned by man this is getting good the word sardine actually refers to many groups of small fishes pilchers sprats and Atlantic herrings mostly young herrings are the primary fishes which makes the array of food fish called sardines timeout so there are no so-called fish named sardines there are actually many groups of small fishes that were captured processed and then labeled sardines pending where they are caught the fish are then denationalized commercialized and advertised as South African sardine Pacific sardine and of course European sardine they're packed without heads or tails naturally being without head and tail who can trace the past status or future of the fish consequently without these identifications sardine is what they are called now the true identity of the fish is legally concealed from the public under the marketing label sardines now watch this not many people notice there is tuna in cans of tuna salmon and cans of salmon mackerel and cans of mackerel what on Earth that was once in the sea is in cans of sardines wow so how does the so-called negro fit into all of this the great God did not create sardines nor placed them in the sea like so the Creator did not create so-called Negroes Indians Chicanos blacks white folks Latinos color people or African Americans Noah placed them on Earth no sub all members of the Human family are indigenous to Earth by divine origin.

[5]

---

5. Elihu N. Pleasant-Bey, *Noble Drew Ali, the Last Prophet: The Exhuming of a Nation* (Seven Seals Publication, 2009).

# The Old Lion and the Fox

An old lion, whose teeth and claws were so worn that it wasn't as easy for him to get food as in his younger days, pretended to be sick. He made sure to inform all his neighbors about it, then laid down in his cave to await visitors. And when they came to offer him their sympathy, he devoured them one by one.

The fox came too, but he was very cautious. He stood at a safe distance from the cave. Politely, he inquired after the lion's health. The lion replied that he was very ill indeed and asked the fox to step inside for a moment. However, Master Fox, very wisely, chose to stay outside. He thanked the lion kindly for the invitation and said, "I would be glad to do as you ask," he added, "but I have noticed that there are many footprints leading into your cave and none coming out. Pray, tell me, how do your visitors find their way out again?"

**Moral:** Take heed of the misfortunes of others. ~Aesop

> Once we collectively stop participating and playing their CORPORATE GAME change will happen overnight.

"I am due in the East right now. I am going to have to go and straighten out the East, and then I will end up in the West. This (The West) will be the easiest. You will be able to be down and sleep, and wake up in peace. This will be, just a breakfast fight. By the time you eat breakfast, it will all be over with."~ Noble Drew Ali[6]

---

6. "Hadith and Prophecies of Noble Drew Ali," in *Califa Uhuru*, 141.

# End Notes

Mahfuz El Bey, Mishaal Talib. *The Torch: A Guide to S.E.L.F.* Califa Media Publishing, 2020.

Meyer, Marvin, trans. *The Secret Teachings of Jesus: Four Gnostic Gospels*. Random House (NY), 1984.

Najee-Ullah El, Tauheedah S, ed. "Hadith and Prophecies of Noble Drew Ali." In *Califa Uhuru: A Compliation of Literature from the Moorish Science Temple of America*, 182. Califa Media Publishing, 2014.

———, ed. "Holy Horan of the Moorish Science Temple of America Circle Seven." In *Califa Uhuru: A Compliation of Literature from the Moorish Science Temple of America*, 55. Califa Media Publishing, 2014.

———, ed. "Koran Questions for Moorish Americans: 101s And Additional Laws." In *Califa Uhuru: A Compliation of Literature from the Moorish Science Temple of America*, 141. Califa Media Publishing, 2014.

Pleasant-Bey, Elihu N. *Noble Drew Ali, the Last Prophet: The Exhuming of a Nation*. Seven Seals Publication, 2009.

## Other Titles from Califa Media Publishing

77 Amazing Facts About the Moors with Complete Proof

(C)over Your Head: A Pictographic Chronology of the Moslem Turban

"Watch My Prophesies:" An Examination of Prophesies from the Prophet Noble Drew Ali

Holistic Philosophy 102

Isonomi: The Great Masonic Secret: Master Keys

Moors in America: A Compilation

Moslem Girls Training Guide: Divinely Prepared for the Sisters' Auxiliary of the Moorish Science Temple of America

Mysteries of the Silent Brotherhood the East aka The Red Book

Nationality: The Order of the Day: Divine Message and Warning, All Garveyites, Rastafarians, Black Nationalists & Pan-Africans

Noble Drew Ali Plenipotentiaries

Official Proclamation of Real Moorish American Nationality

The Holy Koran of the Moorish Holy Temple of Science - 1928 Reprint

The Holy Koran of the Moorish Science Temple of America - Hardcover Edition

The Torch: A Guide to Self

Who Stole the Fez, Moors or Shriners

You Are NOT Negro, Black, Coloured, Morisco, Nor an African Slave

www.ingramcontent.com/pod-product-compliance
Lightning Source LLC
Chambersburg PA
CBHW030156100526
44592CB00009B/306